TIGER
STYLE

TIGER STYLE
Eight Steps to Create a Winning Culture

ISBNs	eBook	979-8-89165-161-6
	Paperback	979-8-89165-162-3
	Hardback	979-8-89165-163-0

Cover Design by Abigael Elliott
Interior Layout and Design by Anton Khodakovsky

Published by
STREAMLINE BOOKS
Kansas City, MO
www.streamlinebookspublishing.com

TIGER STYLE

EIGHT STEPS TO CREATE A WINNING CULTURE

BRIAN SMITH

"Having studied and educated thousands of coaches, I can unequivocally say that Brian Smith is one of the best coaches I have ever met. He is a transformational leader, constantly looking to learn and improve. Whether you are a sports coach, business leader, or leader in another capacity, *Tiger Style* is a must-read. It provides you with a step-by-step method for building a winning team culture."

—DR. DAN GOULD, former director of the Institute for the Study of Youth Sports

"I have worked with Coach Smith for twenty-plus years as the team physician for the University of Missouri wrestling team. He has proven himself to be a winner by creating a great culture and developing young men. Coach Smith has done this by forming Tiger Style. Tiger Style is not just words said when the team breaks a huddle; it is a lifestyle. I have used this framework to build the culture in our practice."

—DR. BUS TARBOX, orthopedic surgeon at Columbia Orthopaedic Group and team physician for Mizzou wrestling since 2001

"Leadership is the result of successes, failures, experiences, vulnerability, and humility. It defines culture, community, and purpose. Brian Smith has captured the essence of servant leadership in *Tiger Style*. This is a 'must-have' tool for any organization that is focused on building and maintaining comprehensive excellence. Outstanding message and strategies!"

—MIKE ALDEN, University of Missouri director of athletics (retired) and principal of MRJ Advisors LLC

"I saw Coach Smith present at a Positive Coaching workshop about the Tiger Style philosophy a few years ago. It was an impressive presentation. Then during the fall semester of 2023, I saw the theory in an applied setting when I worked with the coaches. I witnessed how Coach Smith was open to new ideas and how he interacted with other coaches and athletes. Tiger Style is real. Furthermore, Coach Smith has written this book in an easy-to-follow format with great structure and content. I highly recommend this book to any coach, parent, or athlete."

—BEN LOEB, mental performance consultant to University of Missouri wrestling and Missouri Sports Hall of Fame inductee

"I was blessed to be around when the phrase 'Tiger Style' was adopted. This simply meant we would outwork all the competition. It was a new tradition and standard we set. No shortcuts, no skipping runs, and we always take the stairs. Tiger Style gave us a sense of pride. We upset colleges that hadn't lost to us in decades. We developed the expectation to win with hard work year-round. It is something I look back on proudly as I was part of a culture created, and something I still live today."

—TYRON WOODLEY, two-time All-American and UFC champion

"Tiger Style is a time-tested and championship-proven culture. Coach Smith's approach is inspiring, empowering, and immediately useful in building a winning program. This book gives readers a road map of how Tiger Style works and what drives its effectiveness."

—ELI DRINKWITZ, head football coach at the University of Missouri

To my Father, for being my mentor
and inspiration for coaching and life.

CONTENTS

FOREWORD

MAYBE YOU ARE YOUNG, dreaming, and planning to become a coach. Maybe you are already a coach and now understand the enormous and varied challenges of consistently being a highly effective and successful coach. Maybe you are a veteran coach with a full trophy case and great memories but are still filled with the energy, passion, and belief that there are at least a couple of more great seasons ahead (there's still "gas in your tank"). Or maybe, and most important of all, you are a parent of an athlete of any level of sport, from the first year in youth sports to school sports (elementary, middle school, high school, or collegiate level) to professional sports. If you are *any* of these, then you want the coach to be a great coach. And if you are a parent, it really matters that the coaches are great because they are coaching your kids.

Kids meet Sports at the coach. The coach is the Creator, the Definer, the Shaper, and the Deliverer of the sports experience for every athlete—male/female, big/small, tall/short, fast/slow, experienced/inexperienced, motivated/reticent, etc. And the coach can make or break any kid's sports experience at any time. That is just the truth. If you are the coach, you want to be the Maker, not the Breaker. If you are the parent, you should both want and demand that the coach be the Maker and not the Breaker.

If you are a coach, you should read Coach Brian Smith's book, *Tiger Style*. Parents, you absolutely want to read Coach Smith's book, *Tiger Style*, and then you will want to encourage (demand) that all of your kids' coaches read Coach Brian Smith's book, *Tiger Style*.

There are hundreds of books about the greatest sports coaches of all time, some historic and many current. Some of these books are written *about* the great coach, and some are written *by* those great coaches themselves.

I have read many of these books, featuring coaches such as John Wooden, Tony Dungy, Vince Lombardi, Mike Krzyzewski (Coach K), Pat Summitt, Tara VanDerveer, Phil Jackson, etc. Nearly every book includes the coach's beliefs, principles, and methods. And then there are a growing number of books focused specifically on the processes of coaching: from values and philosophy to building team culture to powerful leadership and motivation.

There are lots of books, and some of these books are great books, great resources. Not one of these books is more important, nor more impactful, than Coach Smith's *Tiger Style!* This is *the* book that aspiring coaches and parents of athletes want, need, and have been waiting to find.

I first met Coach Smith nearly thirty years ago, on his first day on our campus as the University of Missouri Tigers' new head wrestling coach. He was filled with confidence, enthusiasm, and energy, with visions and confidence for building the Tigers wrestling program into a collegiate power. However, the reality was that he had inherited one of the worst programs in the country, consistently at the very bottom of the conference standings. The entire program had been underfunded for years in every aspect: facilities, equipment, recruiting, travel, staff salaries, and so on. There was little hope that things would change much in the foreseeable future.

But Coach Smith had his job, his dream, his opportunity, his vision, his ideas, his work ethic, his motivation and energy, his plan, and his absolute belief that he could outwork everyone else and get the job done. He was a great coach! When he wasn't working, coaching, recruiting, and raising money and support for the program, he invested in learning even more about coaching and leading. He read dozens of those books I previously mentioned. He talked with other coaches, many of whom had faced similar challenges. He regularly walked into my office, sharing questions and ideas, borrowing books from my shelves, and even sitting in my graduate-level sport psychology classes to learn everything he could about the mental aspects of developing athletes and achieving performance at the very highest levels of sports.

Brian's personal belief and recruiting efforts began to see positive results pretty quickly. The program began to move up in the conference standings, a few athletes qualified for the nationals, a few became All-Americans, and he even had his first two national champions. Missouri Tigers wrestling had arrived, the program was respected, and Coach Smith and his Tigers received numerous honors and recognitions for their great achievements. Everyone was happy and celebrated, except Coach Smith.

For sure, he was happy and proud of his athletes and their performances and recognitions. Missouri wrestling was now recognized as a very good program with solid athletes. But Brian knew that there was a big difference between very good and great. He was sure that there was still more in the future for his program, but he couldn't identify exactly what was missing or blocking the way. He examined every aspect of the program, from talent to recruiting to training to health care to scheduling to teaching and coaching. He examined everything. He studied, challenged himself to learn more, and to think "out of the box," beyond the traditional approaches of other successful programs.

At that time, I was teaching a monthly workshop for all of the coaches and support staff in the Mizzou Athletics Department, promoting and encouraging principles of my Power of Positive Coaching program. By the third session, the word had spread, and we had an overflow of attendees in our classroom. It was exciting and encouraging. After a session, Brian held back, waiting for everyone to leave, and then asked if we could have a few minutes so he could show me something.

He began by saying, "I think you are sharing these concepts and principles but want us to see how we can apply them to our own ideas and programs. Is that right?"

Of course, my response was, "That is exactly right!"

Brian smiled and said, "Would you please take a look at what I have to show you, and tell me what you think?"

He opened his folder and showed me pages with diagrams and headings and arrows and figures, all under the heading of "Tiger Style."

He had found his missing piece, and he named it Tiger Style.

And from that day forward, Coach Smith, his coaching staff, support staff, and most importantly his athletes and their families (even their fans)—everyone who lives in or who touches his program—understood and lived with Tiger Style.

Coach Smith's Missouri Tigers wrestling program has won nearly every conference championship since. The team is a perennial challenger for the national championship, and they have produced dozens of All-Americans, several individual national champions, and Olympians. All as a result of living out Tiger Style.

Coach Smith is now a featured speaker throughout the country at coaching conferences and workshops, as well as for corporate and educational settings.

He regularly spoke at my Positive Coaching workshops for high school and collegiate coaches. I have had several nationally recognized speakers in our programs, and Coach Smith's Tiger Style presentation is rated as the very best presentation *every time.*

Coach Smith's book *Tiger Style* is for all coaches and parents of athletes of any age. It is the very best!

—DR. RICK MCGUIRE, Men's and Women's Track &
Field head coach; director, Comprehensive Mental
Performance Program, Department of Intercollegiate
Athletics; graduate professor, Sport Psychology;
founder of the Department of Educational, School, and
Counseling Psychology, Missouri Institute for Positive
Coaching; University of Missouri (Retired)

INTRODUCTION

I'VE GIVEN A LOT OF TALKS at coaching clinics across the United States, and I'm often asked about my reading habits. I do enjoy reading, but it's ironic the way I learned to love it. I learned to love reading as a direct result of getting expelled from English class in fifth grade.

That's right. In fifth grade, I was kicked out of Sister Mary Margaret's English class for being disruptive. As punishment, I was sent to the convent basement. My father happened to be the athletic director and football coach for all the Catholic schools in the area, and he came up with a plan to keep me engaged during my time in the basement. Knowing my love for sports, he suggested that I read *Sports Illustrated* and write reviews or paraphrase the stories. That assignment sparked my love for *Sports Illustrated*, and I remained a subscriber for over thirty-five years until the magazine slowed down and became a monthly publication.

I especially enjoyed reading stories about successful athletes, which ignited my passion for sports. But my interest in reading expanded over time to include history books and biographies. From all of this reading, I began to notice a pattern in the lives of successful people. Specifically, I noticed that successful people always have a vision of what they're trying to achieve, and they work hard to get there.

I often talk about this need for vision with my wrestlers. I encourage my students to openly state their ambitions, whether they dream of becoming an All-American, a national champion, a doctor, or a lawyer, so they know what they're working toward.

Lately, I've been stating my own ambition to write a book, and to my surprise, the people around me have been supportive of the idea. Nobody has called me crazy, and many have even offered to help. In fact, people keep asking me about the progress of my book. For a long time, I had to put them off. "I'm working on it," I would say, but as I've learned, it's a lot harder to write a book than you might imagine. Just getting started feels a bit like trying to climb a mountain. Quite frankly, I wasn't even sure what to write about.

Fortunately, fate intervened when I met a fellow public speaker named Alex Demczak who, along with his colleague Jon Gordon, wrote a book called *The Sale*. Alex suggested that I write about my experiences as a wrestling coach. He even introduced me to a business that assists authors in the writing and publishing process. Despite being busy with coaching, I knew I could no longer put it off. I had all the help I needed, so I finally agreed to write the book. Today, I have fulfilled that commitment.

Now, there is one specific topic that certainly deserves a book of its own, something that is near and dear to my heart. It's a culture and a way of life that we've developed in Mizzou wrestling called "Tiger Style," and it's what we're going to explore in the upcoming chapters.

You might wonder what a wrestling team culture has to do with you (or anyone else, for that matter), but as I've learned through my former students and many others, the values of Tiger Style apply broadly to people in all walks of life. Whether you're a coach, a business leader, a teacher, or something else entirely, you're going to gain insights from my lifetime of learning and coaching that will impact the way you approach life. I believe the best coaches are also the best teachers. It's a sentiment that my father held dear, and this book is a testament to that belief.

THE EIGHT STEPS TO DEVELOPING A TIGER STYLE CULTURE

Not long ago, I was contacted by a local radio station, KMOX, for an interview. They had heard about this thing called Tiger Style, and they wanted to discuss it. In a way, it reminded them of the "Cardinal Way" culture of the MLB Cardinals. They even flattered me by calling my wrestling program the most successful college sports program in Missouri.

Well, how could I say no? With the limited timeframe of the interview, I knew I had to come up with a way to concisely articulate what Tiger Style is all about. So, I sat down and began organizing our culture into eight steps that I felt were the heart and soul of what we're all about. I poured my heart into preparing for the interview. It felt a bit reminiscent of my younger days as an athlete, gearing up for a big match.

After that interview, the "Eight Steps of Tiger Style" became a speech that I gave to over 300 supporters at a golf outing dinner. Despite the attendees being a little under the influence of the alcohol provided on the course, the talk was well received, with the entire audience standing up to applaud at the end. It felt like the reaction of an enthusiastic crowd when a wrestler pins someone in a dual meet at Mizzou's Hearnes Center.

Driving home, I called my wife, Denise, and told her that it was one of my better talks. All I did was share about Tiger Style, and they loved it. It made me realize that I needed to share this with more people because it seems to resonate, and more importantly, Tiger Style works. It works for all kinds of people.

In fact, no matter where you're coming from, I am confident that you will see how living Tiger Style can benefit you as a coach, as a business leader, as a teacher, or simply as a human being.

CHAPTER 1

KNOWING YOUR IDENTITY

WHERE DID THIS THING called Tiger Style come from? How did it become such an intrinsic part of the wrestling team at Mizzou?

Picture the end of a grueling practice session. The team huddles, arms raised, breaking down the day's triumphs and trials. Then, a voice rings out, "Tiger Style on three! One, two, three, Tiger Style!" This ritual was introduced by Jeremy Spates, a member of my first recruiting class at Mizzou in 1999, who is now the head coach of wrestling at Southern Illinois University Edwardsville. His high school team was also called the Tigers, so this breakdown was a familiar tradition that he brought along with him.

Fast forward to 2002, our breakout season. We were at the Virginia Duals, a dual meet tournament, and we had made it to the finals. Before heading over to the tournament, I asked my assistants to jot down the team's thoughts. I gathered the team, their faces filled with excitement, and posed a question: "Guys, we always end by chanting 'Tiger Style,' but what does Tiger Style mean to you?"

The team responded with a flurry of ideas. It's a lifestyle, some said. It means punctuality. It's about hard work. They gave me a list of thirty or forty things that defined their perception of Tiger Style. That was the beginning of writing Tiger Style down on paper. We ended up winning that dual 25-to-13, finished the season 18-and-3, and I knew I had to get Tiger Style written down. It needed to become something concrete to build on the energy and excitement of that winning season, something that could keep the momentum going in future seasons.

Other people heard us talking about Tiger Style. As I started speaking at rotary clubs and different groups around Columbia and the state, I was often asked, "What is Tiger Style?"

Ultimately, I broke down Tiger Style into four pillars: **Believe, Compete, One More**, and **Expect to Win**. These four things encapsulate the virtues, values, and lifestyle I was constantly trying to instill in my wrestlers. I will be speaking about them throughout this book.

Of course, I didn't form Tiger Style in a vacuum. I have been shaped and influenced by many people myself over the years. I've read many books by inspirational coaches like Vince Lombardi, John Wooden, Pete Carroll, and Mike "Coach K" Krzyzewski. My dad, who was my mentor and a coach himself, played a huge role in shaping me. From the time I was a young kid, about five or six years old, my dad would take me on the sidelines, into the coaches' meeting rooms, and to coaches' clinics. We would sit at home and break down sports films. He taught me what it really means to be a coach, and I loved it. I knew that was my passion and what I would become.

I began to infuse Tiger Style into everything I did as a coach. We even started calling our wrestling camps "Tiger Style Camps," and wow, did they grow. From the early 2000s to 2010, they grew so big we were getting close to 2,000 kids in three weeks of camp. And every single kid who came through the camp got a shirt that said "Tiger Style."

I would see those camp shirts all over the place. I remember walking through the Atlanta airport and seeing some kids wearing them. People were seeing Tiger Style everywhere, and they were talking about it.

The four pillars of Tiger Style (Believe, Compete, One More, and Expect to Win) made it easier than ever to share what it meant, and we began to gather stories of the ways it was impacting former camp kids and wrestlers later in their lives. As our fan base and the Mizzou administration observed the way our team members behaved, presented themselves, took on leadership roles, and pursued degree programs, they began to ask about it.

Our program started to have purpose and direction through Tiger Style. I added a team mantra that was perfect for where we were going. The speech I borrowed this from was the September 12, 1962, speech by President John F. Kennedy. President Kennedy had to convince the country to invest billions of dollars in trying to get to the moon. There were so many more immediate problems in our country that going to the moon was a tough sell. Many did not believe we could do it, and the Russians were already close to achieving it first. However, in his inspiring speech, Kennedy talked about the human spirit and having the vision and drive to try to achieve the most difficult tasks.

I continue to use my speech to motivate the team as well as the businesses and groups I speak to. It shows the importance of having a vision and working for it. Whether that vision is trying to go to the moon or winning a championship, it can be achieved.

Here is our program mantra.

WHY CHOOSE TIGER STYLE?

We choose Tiger Style as a lifestyle, not because it is easy, but because it is hard. We choose Tiger Style because its goals and expectations will serve to organize and measure the best of our energies and skills, because that challenge is one that we are willing to accept, one we are unwilling to postpone, and one we Expect To Win.

As Tiger Style took root in our program, I began receiving frequent emails from people in the community praising our young men for their outstanding behavior and the lifestyle they chose to live. I would always forward these emails to the administration, and they would respond, "We love that your guys are living Tiger Style." The team was winning, and they were graduating with high-level degrees. Momentum was growing, and word was spreading.

THE BATTLE FOR TIGER STYLE

Of course, no good thing can gain traction without overcoming a few obstacles along the way. As Tiger Style grew, people started telling me that I needed to copyright the phrase "Tiger Style." They argued that it should be *my* phrase since it was associated with my camps, and I had come up with it and defined the four pillars. I was initially skeptical of this idea, but I eventually decided to do it. Scott Tarbox, a lawyer in Denver and the brother of my team doctor, helped me with the copyrighting process. He submitted all the paperwork to the government, which then had to be posted for a certain period to check for any copyright interference.

On the very last day, lawyers in Atlanta representing the University of Missouri contacted us and claimed that I couldn't use the word "Tiger." This led to a six-month battle with the administration and their lawyers over who owned the rights to the words. Despite their adamant refusal and my evidence showing that I had been using "Tiger Style" for my private camps under my LLC, the debate continued.

To me, Tiger Style was synonymous with Mizzou wrestling, so I didn't want it to be appropriated and lose its significance. In the midst of this legal dispute, the chancellor of the University of

Missouri sent out an email to all students during the first week of school, inviting them to a "Tiger Style Barbecue" on Saturday. I was taken aback. Here he was using those exact words in the middle of our protracted copyright battle.

I received several emails from people in the athletic department, unaware of the ongoing legal battle, jokingly urging me to confront the chancellor for trying to steal my words. I was upset, so I approached the administration and expressed my concerns. This misuse would dilute the value of the word and ruin its purpose, which was to represent the culture of Mizzou wrestling.

As we neared the end of the dispute, we all sat down for a discussion. In the end, the administration agreed to let me use the words, but they would be owned by the University of Missouri Athletics and reserved for wrestling.

So, we didn't win outright. "Tiger Style" is technically controlled by the University of Missouri Athletics, and we have a copyright that says it can only be used for Mizzou wrestling. The cherry on top is that the university administration had to pay my legal fees. We actually ended up with a nice sum of money, all of which was donated to our program.

And that, my friends, was the battle for "Tiger Style." It soon became the culture of our program and our true identity.

EVERYONE PLAYS A PART

When I speak to recruits for the wrestling team at Mizzou, they almost always ask, "What is Tiger Style?" I take them through the four pillars: Believe, Compete, One More, and Expect to Win.

This explanation has made it easier for everyone on our staff and those close to the program to understand what Tiger Style is. Fans, alumni, administration, and even high school coaches have learned it and adopted it. I've given many talks about it at

Mizzou, and most of the other coaches have come to my office to learn about our culture. When I hire new staff, I expect them to live up to those standards and uphold the culture.

Tiger Style is more than a catchphrase or a set of ideas. It is an encapsulation of our identity at Mizzou wrestling, and if I've learned anything over my years as a coach, it's that you must figure out who you are and what you're all about if you're going to achieve anything significant in life.

To be clear, knowing who you are doesn't guarantee success. Just because you read this book and follow it doesn't guarantee that you're going to be a national champion. It doesn't work that way, and not everything is controllable. However, when you, your team, and your organization believe in doing things a certain way, live the culture, continuously seek ways to grow and improve, and demand accountability from yourself and others, it will greatly increase your chances for success. That's what this book is about.

I heard a story recently about a man whose brother was battling cancer. His brother's goal was to stay alive long enough to witness the birth of his child, so he sought treatment at MD Anderson Cancer Center in Houston. During one of his visits to his brother, the man decided to walk around the hospital.

He approached the front desk and asked the staff about their roles. To his surprise, every staff member, regardless of their actual position, responded the same. When he asked, "What do you do here?" they replied, "I cure cancer." He even encountered a janitor mopping the floor and asked him the same question. The janitor, too, responded with, "I cure cancer." From the receptionist to the doctors and nurses, everyone said the same thing.

Excited, the man rushed back to his brother and shared his discovery. This unified sense of purpose resonated with him.

Everyone associated with the hospital, regardless of their specific tasks or roles, was committed to the mission of curing cancer.

That's a great example of what it looks like when culture is a lifestyle, not just a catchphrase.

When I share this story with my team, I emphasize that everyone in our wrestling room, from our strength coach and academic advisor to our wrestlers, coaches, and team doctor, must be committed to living Tiger Style. Our goal is not only to win a national title but also to live Tiger Style every day, which means every person doing the right things to achieve greatness in life. As Vince Lombardi put it, "The question is usually not how well each person performs, but how well they work together."

Every wrestler on my team understands that each individual must contribute. Whether they are the returning national champ or the fourth-stringer on the team, they must live Tiger Style, and in doing so, they are helping us win a national title. Just like every worker in a cancer hospital is doing everything they possibly can in their specific role to help cure cancer, every wrestler has to do everything they can to give us the best possible chance to succeed.

What makes Tiger Style so effective is that it gives every member of the wrestling program a crystal clear identity and purpose. This is something many teams, not to mention organizations and individuals, lack. What makes you and your organization successful? What are you all about? Figure that out, and embody it every day, not just during practice or competition. Instill it in every team member, every employee, and let it shape your culture, influencing how you act, react, and communicate with each other.

Knowing your identity propels you toward your purpose by helping you recognize your strengths and leverage them to excel. This is a lesson I impart to my team. Of course, it's equally important to acknowledge your weaknesses. To address this, I hire people who can complement my strengths and help mitigate my weaknesses.

I often tell my team that we don't have to do anything extraordinary when we compete. Just do the ordinary exceptionally well. By doing what *you* do best—which comes from knowing your identity—you give yourself a chance to fulfill your purpose. Whether it's stepping on a mat to win a match or becoming a doctor, you need to know your strengths.

THE MARK ELLIS STORY

I tried to recruit Mark Ellis for wrestling right out of high school, but he turned me down. Instead, he said he decided to walk on for football at Mizzou. When he arrived, I made a pact with the assistant football coach, Andy Hill, that if Mark didn't make it in football, I would take him for wrestling.

A few weeks into practice, Andy called me up and said Mark wasn't going to make it in football. So, I took Mark and pulled him out for wrestling. His first year was a disaster. He struggled academically *and* athletically, and he seemed lost. We managed to save him from flunking out and convinced him to give us another year. We moved him in with Ben Askren, a future two-time Dan Hodge Trophy winner, and started talking to him about living Tiger Style.

Over the course of his redshirt freshman year, Mark started to improve and said he believed he could become a national champion. I told him that if he truly believed it, he had to work at it every day. Bear in mind, he was unable to beat anyone in the room at the time, but he kept coming back and getting better. His sophomore year saw further improvement, but he lost in the All-American round and was devastated.

In his junior year, Mark kept fighting and improving, eventually ranking in the top five in the country. However, he lost in the Big 12 finals and once again felt crushed. I reminded him of other wrestlers who had lost in the Big 12 finals but went on to win the national title. I encouraged him to wipe his tears, get back to work, and prepare for the nationals. Mark went on to win every match and clinch the 2009 NCAA title. It's an amazing story of perseverance and belief.

He also changed his life and found faith. He's now one of the top leaders for Fellowship of Christian Athletes and oversees FCA wrestling for the entire country. He often gives talks, encouraging people to live for a purpose in life. Think about how far he came. Here was a young man who almost walked away from everything, almost flunked out and gave up, but he became an NCAA title winner who continues to inspire other people to live great lives and accomplish great things.

Here is Mark's side of the story:

MARK'S STORY: **WHO BELIEVES IN YOU?**

Believing in yourself is important, but so is who believes in you. Who is speaking into your life, and what are they saying? It matters what words you are speaking about yourself and those around you, but it's just as important what the people closest to you are speaking into your life.

Most of us have heard the saying "You become the average of those closest to you." This is why we cannot *drift* into relationships; we must choose them wisely. Although I believe you must choose the people you spend the most time with wisely, I thank God for the people He allowed into my life at just the right time.

Just before my freshman year of college, I thought I wanted to quit wrestling and attend a smaller college, and possibly even switch sports to football. Most of the people I was drifting toward did not aspire to win national championships, but I had a coach and a teammate who saw and spoke differently into my life.

I was discouraged and overwhelmed, so it was difficult to see or imagine the journey ahead. However, I was blessed to have these people in my life who could see my potential. I remember the call I received from Ben Askren telling me he had an extra room in his house for me. He informed me rather firmly that I wasn't quitting and insisted that we have a sit-down talk about what was going on and what could be ahead if I continued to wrestle. I received another phone call from Ben's dad, Chuck, telling me something similar.

And then I received a phone call from Coach Smith inviting me into his office for the sit-down meeting that Ben may have been referring to. Coach Smith and Ben were both in Coach's office waiting for me to arrive. I remember a few things from that meeting, but mostly I remember Coach and Ben speaking "life" into me. They wanted me to change my living arrangements and move into Ben's house. I agreed, and everything changed from that moment on.

From the day I showed up at Mizzou, I started saying I wanted to win a national championship. There were many moments of difficulty and doubt, but I continued to speak it to anyone who asked and would listen. I didn't go around boasting, "I'm going to win a national championship," but if anyone asked me what I believed for myself, I didn't hesitate to tell them. In doing so, I was building myself up by speaking my goal over and over again.

Getting there, of course, required a whole lot of work over a long period of time. There were days I would come home from practice, then turn right around and put in another workout. We had a wrestling room in the basement of our house. Often, we would come home, eat dinner, then immediately go down to the basement for another workout. Some days, we drilled and went over positions I needed to get better in. Other days, we would set a clock for a certain amount of time and just wrestle. There were many tough workouts in that wrestling room in the basement and many tough conversations about pushing through adversity and limitations.

Speaking life and continuing to say the right things, regardless if things are going as planned, is incredibly important to achieving our goals, but we also have to do the work behind the words.

When I ran out onto the stage for the NCAA National Championship match, doubts tried to run through my head one more time before the dream could become a reality. However, when doubt showed up, I looked over to see the people who had spoken life and believed in me, and they stood in my corner again. The negative thoughts disappeared, and thoughts of gratitude began to flood my mind. I felt grateful for my health, grateful for those God had put in my life, and grateful for the opportunity presented to me.

These are lessons I carry with me today. What am I speaking over myself, my family, and those God has put in my life? Whom do I allow to speak into my life? Words are powerful. I believe they are more important than most people realize. They are often the rudder that steers the ship, setting you on a certain course. Commit to speaking life and saying the right things. Then put these words into action. And then you will start to truly believe!

–Mark Ellis

Mark Ellis's story reminds me of something Bill Walsh, former coach of the San Francisco 49ers, said in his book *The Score Takes Care of Itself.* In the book, Walsh emphasizes the importance of creating the highest operating standards, developing the character of young players, and fostering a team culture. He believes that when these elements are in place, "the score will take care of itself."

This philosophy aligns perfectly with the essence of Tiger Style. In our culture, we set high standards that revolve around belief, competition, and the drive to go one step further. With these standards, there's an expectation to win. But it's all about developing character. By cultivating a strong team culture that develops character, you set the stage for success, and it all begins with figuring out who you are.

GARBAGE CAN INTRODUCTION

When I got my first job as a history teacher at Western High School in Fort Lauderdale, I felt extremely nervous. It was my first time being fully in charge of a classroom, so I sought advice from my dad, who had been teaching for over thirty-five years. He suggested a rather unconventional approach for my first day of teaching.

"When you first get to your classroom, grab a metal garbage can," he said. "Once all the students are inside, throw the garbage can across the floor to make a lot of noise. Then introduce yourself as their teacher and lay down the law."

I was taken aback by his intense approach. This was a classroom, after all. But he insisted that I needed to show the kids that I was the boss.

So finally, the first day of the semester arrived, and I found myself standing outside the classroom, holding a metal garbage can. As I watched the young freshmen come in, the bell rang. I prepared myself to walk in and throw the garbage can—just as my dad had recommended—but then it hit me: This wasn't me. This was my dad's approach, not mine.

My identity was such that I could talk to these kids, relate to them. While I had learned a lot from my dad and was an intense person myself, I wasn't him. Yes, it's important to learn from your mentors—and my father was certainly a mentor to me—but you also have to develop your own identity.

So, I walked in, set the garbage can down, introduced myself as Coach Smith, wrote my name on the board, and started getting to know the students. I asked them to tell me about themselves. I ended up having a great time teaching. The students enjoyed me as a teacher and as a person they could relate to. I'm really glad I decided to be myself and not throw that garbage can.

You have to discover your own identity and purpose. It's a learning process that often includes observing how others live, discerning what works for you and what doesn't, and incorporating the best aspects into your own life.

During my college years, I had coaches who taught me valuable lessons, not only about how to coach but also about how *not* to coach. My coach at Michigan State during my freshman year was Pat Milkovich. Pat knew I wanted to coach, so he pushed me to learn not only as an athlete but also for when I would become a coach. At summer camp after my first season, he told me to get into the hip pocket of a top high school coach who was working there. I ate with the coach, I was there when he was teaching, and I took notes on his teaching and his advice. I even observed how he communicated with the athletes. My identity evolved out of these experiences, and my purpose was defined by the wrestling program I later developed.

Life is a continuous learning process. We learn from our mistakes as well as our successes. By taking all these experiences and lessons, I was able to find my own unique approach. In fact, I believe Tiger Style represents the culmination of my life's learning and experiences. It is my identity *and* my purpose.

Now, *you* have to figure out who *you* are and what *your* purpose is. From there, you can help your team, your students, your employees, your family—and whoever else—discover theirs.

I've used exercises over the years to help my wrestlers and camp kids discover their own identities and embrace their purpose. I'll share two with you.

EXERCISE 1: **WHAT DO THEY SAY ABOUT US?**

This is an exercise I've done many times with my wrestlers. It could work for any athletic program, and it could work for a business, a team, or any other group of people who are trying to clarify and live out their culture.

I'll bring my team together and present them with the following question: "Ideally, what would another coach or a competitor say are the qualities of Tiger Style?" This encourages them to try to see themselves from another perspective. They will then come up with a list of things, like hardworking, intense, aggressive, great fan support, and so on.

I make a list of their responses. Then I break them up into small groups. Each group takes one of the items on the list, and they discuss what actions we need to take to support that quality. For example, if one of the items on the list is "family friendly," then that group needs to determine what actions Mizzou wrestling needs to take (or what things we need to *stop* doing) in order to embody being "family friendly." If one of the items is "aggressive," then they might come up with some ideas for practices that are designed to develop toughness and intensity.

If you conduct this meeting at the beginning of the week, you can put the actions into practice over the course of the week. Turn the theoretical into the practical. It's a good way to help your team define and refine their identity and connect it to concrete actions.

EXERCISE 2: *BEING UNCOMMON*

When I work with businesses, I often conduct an exercise in which we explore what makes someone "uncommon," which is a key aspect of developing an identity. During the exercise, I ask participants to think of individuals who stand out to them as being uncommon. Responses often include famous athletes, but I also highlight figures like Mother Teresa, who chose an uncommon path by dedicating fifty years of her life to caring for the terminally ill.

Of course, uncommon also extends to having ambitious goals, such as climbing the highest mountain or becoming an astronaut. These are not common paths, and not everyone gets to achieve them.

To delve deeper into this concept, I then divide participants into four groups. Each group tackles one of these questions:

1. What makes someone uncommon?
2. Why do people choose to climb the highest mountain (or whatever uncommon goal you want to use)?
3. If you chose to climb the highest mountain, what would you need to be successful?
4. Why do some people choose not to climb the highest mountain?

Each group will then spend five to ten minutes brainstorming and preparing to present their findings to the entire group.

This exercise sparks a rich discussion on developing an identity and purpose. For example, if the goal is to climb the highest mountain, the reasons might vary from personal achievement to lifelong ambition. The resources needed could range from physical equipment to mentors.

This exercise can be applied to any goal, such as building a successful company. By going through these steps and breaking into groups, participants can start to develop and understand their unique identity.

CHAPTER 2

THE SMALL THINGS WIN

THE WEEK BEFORE conferences and the NCAA Championships, I am often reminded of my time as a high school coach. During my first year, coaches from a bunch of different schools wanted to organize joint practices since only a few of their athletes had qualified for the state tournament. The majority of my team qualified, so I was hesitant about these joint sessions. Nevertheless, I invited the other teams to practice with us since they only had a few athletes each.

I quickly noticed that their approach differed from mine. The other coaches suggested special high-intensity, competitive workouts, but I knew that wasn't what we needed. Instead, I believed in refining and reinforcing what we'd already been practicing all season. My philosophy, which I inherited from my father, was to bring the focus back to the fundamentals, especially during critical times of the year. As the season reached its peak, the most important thing we could do was to perfect what we'd already worked on consistently.

I still discuss this with my coaching staff and team as we approach the championship season each year. I ask them to identify the most important aspects of our preparation. The consensus is always the same: wrestle within themselves, execute their individual game plans, execute the basics, and be proficient at taking down and controlling their opponents.

All of their preparation throughout the year is what truly

counts. They don't need to do anything extraordinary when conference looms; they just need to keep doing what they've been doing all along. This mindset carries into our practice sessions, which focus on drills and techniques.

I'm a firm believer that the fundamentals are the foundation of success. The small things win, not some special, secret technique applied at the last minute. Mastering the basics and consistently applying them is what leads to victory.

TAKING THE STAIRS

Ironically, when I first took over the wrestling program at Mizzou, there were rumors of potentially dropping the program altogether. The team had been struggling for years, both on and off the mat. The wrestlers generally had low GPAs, there were issues within the community, and their behavior didn't reflect the values of a successful team. They were consistently at the bottom of the conference, unable to excel in any aspect. To put it bluntly, they were simply not good at anything worthwhile.

I had my work cut out for me, and I had to figure out where to start to turn things around. It seemed to me the first thing we needed to do was to instill some small, positive habits in the team members that would foster a mindset of success and eventually lead us to victory. The opportunity to begin this transformation came in the form of a simple decision: Everyone was going to start taking the stairs instead of the elevator.

At that time, our practice facility was on the fourth floor, and on my first day as coach, I made the fateful decision to take the stairs. I decided this would be mandatory for my wrestlers. Every day, they were to take the stairs to practice. Despite some initial complaints from the team, this soon became ingrained in our program's culture. Taking the stairs became a symbol of our commitment to doing things the better way, not necessarily the easy way.

Years passed, and the tradition endured. Former team members would return, proudly proclaiming that they still took the stairs. It became a mindset—a belief that you could achieve anything if you were willing to put in a little extra hard work and not cut corners for the sake of convenience and ease.

In the wrestling room, I enforced a similar principle. For example, when my wrestlers were running laps in the practice room, I required them to run *around* the circles on the mat instead of cutting across. This might seem like a small thing— and it is—but these kinds of small things laid the foundation for our program's eventual growth and success. We will not cut corners to be successful in this program.

Over the years, as we've accumulated countless steps on those stairs, I've watched the impact of this idea really take root and grow. What has become clear to me is that success isn't always about winning matches—it's about embracing a mindset of continuous improvement, one step at a time.

ONE MORE

Another rule I created was called "One More," which meant pushing beyond what was required in practice. As I told the guys, "Do what is required of you, and then do one more." This rule, which is now one of the four pillars of Tiger Style, is meant to instill the idea that excellence isn't achieved through minimum effort but through consistently going above and beyond.

Don't settle for doing what everyone else is doing. Find ways to do more, to do a little extra, whether that's taking the stairs instead of the elevator, or putting in extra practice late at night or early in the morning.

The story behind One More actually began one day when I was eating lunch in the practice room. One of my assistant coaches was training for the Olympic trials with a freshman on the team. They were the only ones on the mat, and as I watched, I saw my assistant coach, a high-level competitor, struggling against the freshman. The young wrestler was confident and managed to take down the coach several times.

At one point, the coach called out, "Let's go two more." In those final two rounds, my assistant coach regained control and won both times. The freshman, visibly upset, grabbed his headgear and stormed out of the room without a word. The assistant coach came over to me, frustrated that the freshman couldn't see his own progress and instead focused on the last two takedowns.

Suddenly, the freshman burst back into the room, looked directly at the coach, and declared, "We're going one more." That moment of determination was powerful. I quickly jotted down the significance of that attitude: the willingness to push yourself beyond the point of giving up, to always strive for that extra effort to improve.

I realized that if everyone in our program adopted this mindset, it would lead to significant improvements. If our team, coaches, academic advisors, and even our support staff all committed to making one more phone call, completing one more repetition in practice or the weight room, putting in one more effort, it would collectively enhance our performance across the board.

This concept of doing one more extends beyond physical effort. I also emphasize to my team the importance of doing a little more in regard to their appearance and attitude. A championship team should look and behave like champions. This means dressing in our team apparel, always speaking positively, and taking pride in our facilities. For example, instead of saying, "I suck today," they should reframe it as, "I was challenged today, and I will get back on the mat and improve." Maintaining a clean and organized facility is another aspect of doing a little more to show pride and commitment.

I illustrate this to the guys using the analogy of a well-kept neighborhood. A poorly maintained house stands out in a bad way, just as a disorganized team facility would. We never want to project an image of carelessness or a lack of commitment. We always want to show, to ourselves and others, that we go above and beyond and have a championship facility.

Moreover, we always try to end each day on a positive note. If practice is tough, I encourage the team to stay a bit longer, work on their weaknesses, and try to leave feeling accomplished. This attitude started rippling through their interactions, improving their mood and their relationships with teammates, family, and friends. We call this "end the day with a positive."

All these small, daily actions contributed to building a championship attitude and mindset, which is essential for achieving goals and enjoying success.

PUTTING ON YOUR SOCKS

In wrestling, you can never afford to stop learning. As soon as you master a move, your opponents will develop a countermove. You have to refine and adapt constantly, so you can't become satisfied with being "good enough." You must always strive to improve.

At the beginning of each season, I share a story with the team about John Wooden, the legendary UCLA basketball coach. On the first day of practice, Wooden would teach his players something seemingly trivial: how to put on their athletic socks properly. This might sound absurd, but it had an important purpose. Among other things, he showed them how to make sure the socks were smooth and crease-free in order to prevent blisters, because blisters can lead to missed practices. It was a simple lesson that highlighted the importance of even the smallest details in maintaining team continuity and performance.

This attention to detail is what I emphasize constantly in our practice room. Every little thing matters, from how you put on your socks to how you perform each move. This is the essence of a championship mindset. Vince Lombardi, one of the greatest football coaches of all time, always started his opening day of practice by showing his players a football, saying, "Gentlemen, this is a football," and drilling them on the basic fundamentals of the game. His focus on fundamentals and small details paved the way for success. You never graduate past the basics. Yes, you build on them, but you never move past them.

I also draw inspiration from Admiral William McRaven's book *Make Your Bed*. As McRaven always says, completing a small task, like making your bed each morning, sets a positive tone for the rest of the day. This initial small accomplishment encourages further productivity, which creates a chain reaction of completed tasks. It's a philosophy that lies at the foundation of our approach: Mastering small tasks leads to bigger achievements.

We have two fundamental team rules: (1) attend every class and (2) live Tiger Style. The latter encompasses all the unwritten expectations we hold. One example is taking those fifty-four stairs up to the fourth-floor practice room twice a day, six days a week, which adds up to 50,000 steps annually. It's a small, consistent effort that accumulates into huge results.

The problem is too many people focus solely on the big end goal without paying attention to the small, immediate tasks that they can accomplish now. It's a common problem, and I think it stems from the way success is often portrayed. Consider diet ads. They always show the dramatic before and after pictures, but they never show the months or years of effort in between. The hard work, discipline, and small daily sacrifices required to achieve those weight loss results are glossed over in favor of a quick-fix narrative.

This tendency to overlook the process sometimes makes it difficult for people to stay focused. It's much easier to dream about the end result than to commit to the daily grind. For example, cooking a delicious homemade dinner involves a long process of preparation, not just the quick convenience of a microwave meal. The same principle applies in sports and business: Develop good habits, focus on doing the small things well, and practice consistently.

In the 2024 NBA finals, I heard a Boston Celtic answer the question, "What will you remember most about this championship?" His answer outlines the secret to success: "Just the whole process. We didn't skip any steps from the beginning to the end."

As part of this focus on our team, I always stress the importance of showing up and being present. That means going to class, writing thank-you notes, and maintaining personal connections. In business, a handwritten thank-you note is a small thing that can make a significant impact compared to a quick email. Similarly, calling boosters or customers just to check in on them, rather than to make a sale, builds strong, lasting relationships. These are small things that accumulate to big results.

By focusing on the small tasks consistently, we achieve big goals. It's through our daily actions and disciplined habits that we lay the foundation for long-term success.

EXERCISE: **WHAT ARE YOUR HABITS?**

One exercise I do to help my wrestling team focus on the small things is to talk to them about their habits. I ask them what their daily habits are without getting too detailed initially. For instance, I ask them about their morning routines. Do they make their bed, brush their teeth, and eat breakfast?

Then we discuss the benefits of these good habits. Brushing your teeth daily ensures better hygiene and long-term dental health. Eating a nutritious breakfast can significantly impact your performance throughout the day. Conversely, skipping breakfast can hinder athletic performance.

We also talk about how their daily habits contribute to success. Our team rule of attending every class is one example. By consistently going to class, athletes absorb information, engage with peers, and develop a disciplined routine. This habit reinforces their commitment to their goals.

Through all of this, I challenge the team to examine their small, routine actions and determine whether those actions align with their beliefs and goals. For example, hitting the snooze button might seem harmless, but it can hinder progress by promoting a lack of discipline. On the other hand, getting up as soon as the alarm rings can set a positive tone for the day.

The goal is to show how our small daily habits contribute to our success. If a wrestler wants to become a national champion, he can't afford to be late to practice or miss training sessions.

This principle is just as true in the business world as it is in a college athletic program. For example, a sales rep might set a goal of making twenty calls a day and commit to sticking with it, even on nice, sunny days when the distractions are many. It's a small commitment that will accumulate over the months and years into big success. Maybe they could also commit to following up those calls with thank-you notes and consistent communication.

The goal is to get your team members to identify the daily habits and small things that will build toward big, long-term success. Help them see how taking small, consistent actions lays the foundation for achieving larger goals.

CHAPTER 3

FOCUS ON WHAT YOU HAVE (NOT WHAT OTHERS HAVE)

URING THE SECOND semester of my first year at Missouri, we went to Oklahoma State for a dual meet. I was eager to see how my team would compete against such a big, successful school. However, the moment we stepped into their practice room the day before the dual, I could sense my team's confidence wavering. They were awestruck by the room's display of Olympians, NCAA champions, and All-Americans. Their admiration quickly turned into intimidation.

The sense of intimidation intensified when we entered Gallagher-Iba Arena. The imposing crowd, the thirty-something national championship banners hanging down, and the overwhelming atmosphere were too much for my team. They were defeated by the environment even before they stepped onto the mat. The looks on their faces said it all.

For me, this experience highlighted the need to cultivate a strong belief in our own program and identity. It wasn't an easy process, but through small, consistent actions, we began to build that belief. Our team GPA improved as players started going to class regularly. Taking the stairs became a metaphor for the hard-work mentality that was taking root in our program. Our talent level started to rise, and the same guys who were on the team that went 4-9-0 in duals in 1999 began to believe in the work they were putting in, the habits they were developing, and the lifestyle they were embracing.

In the summer of 2001, after three challenging seasons with a 22-30 record in dual meets, I knew the team had potential despite our lack of success. We worked diligently all summer, focusing on the details and the extra efforts—those "One Mores"—that would eventually pay off. The belief within the team continued to grow. As the season approached, I plastered signs all over the facility with the phrase "Expect to Win." I didn't promise victories, but I wanted the team to develop a winning attitude.

This mindset marked a significant shift in our performance. My fourth team at Mizzou was the first that didn't care about the other team's ranking or their banners and fancy facilities. They were prepared to compete at the highest level, and their body language showed it. We opened the season against the ninth-ranked team, Illinois, and won six out of ten matches. Impressively, three of those matches went into overtime, and we won all three. This could have easily gone the other way, but their expectation to win and their confident mindset carried them through.

That season we finished 18-3, which was a big turning point for our program. Since then, we have not had a losing season. This transformation came from focusing on what we could control, improving ourselves, letting the little things accumulate into a championship mindset, and not being intimidated by what another team might have.

A SELF-DEFEATING ATTITUDE

So many people in sports, in business, and in life focus on what others have that they lack, but this is a self-defeating attitude. I have tried to explain this to my wife using a personal story. When we lived in our previous home, we had a neighbor who was an exceptional landscaper. My wife often pointed out how well kept and extravagant Tom's yard looked compared to ours, and I would remind her that I was a successful wrestling coach, not a landscaper. I told her to either stop comparing or start landscaping. She ended up hiring a service to improve our yard, but we spent a lot of money in the process. I don't think I won in this situation.

The problem with comparing ourselves to others is that it wastes time, and it can bring us down. This attitude can ruin your motivation and confidence, much like it did for our team at Oklahoma State in 1999. No one has it perfect, and what you see may not be the full picture. Every team, every business, and every place has its issues. It's far better to focus on what you do have and build from there.

When I first arrived at Missouri, our wrestling facility on the fourth floor was a big mess. The walls were painted an ugly army green, and the outside room was used as a storage area. We shared offices, and the facility was the smallest in the Big 12. Despite this, I knew we had to change the perception of our practice space. I started calling it the "penthouse" of the Hearnes Center since it was on the top floor. People immediately associated the term "penthouse" with luxury, and it changed not only my mindset but also that of my team and others.

We began making small improvements, like painting the walls a nicer color, cleaning, and adding graphics. Over the years, our facility improved, and eventually, Mizzou built a new arena, allowing us to take over the basketball practice gym, which made our practice facility one of the largest and nicest in the country. This transformation didn't happen overnight, but it started with the penthouse mentality.

The key is to view obstacles as opportunities instead of problems. It's almost a childlike mindset. Let's suppose you have a big, empty cardboard box sitting in the middle of the room. A child will see that cardboard box as a source of endless possibilities and fun, while an adult will see it as trash that needs to be discarded. We have to adopt that child-like perspective to see the potential in every situation.

Our poor facilities weren't the only problem I had to confront as the new head coach at Mizzou. I also had to deal with low pay, no paid second assistant, and a last-place team. Our uniforms were old, our budget was minimal, and most of the athletic department had written off the program entirely. Honestly, when they hired me at such a minimal salary, I think they were hoping I'd fail so they could justify dropping the program. But I knew all that and didn't waste time worrying about it. Instead, I focused on finding ways to get people excited about Missouri wrestling.

I started telling everyone I met about the program and adding them to a mailing list. I spoke to civic groups, Rotary Clubs, and anyone who would listen. Twenty-six years later, I met a guy who remembered my first year. He said, "You came to my Rotary Club and had this powerful vision of what you were trying to build. The program has become that vision." I told him, "Well, almost. We haven't won nationals yet, but we're getting there. Our program is much better."

Instead of complaining about what we lacked, I focused on finding talent. I traveled around the state doing free clinics and getting to know high school coaches. As I said, we found inexpensive ways to improve the facility, like painting the walls. We had no money, but we knew that wasn't changing anytime soon. So, we built up our summer camps. My staff and I built some of the biggest camps in the Midwest. In the early 2000s, we had close to 2,000 kids coming through our camps in three weeks. The money from these camps helped pay my assistants and me, sometimes matching our salaries because our regular pay was so low.

These camps not only supplemented our salaries but also built relationships with coaches throughout the state. Through our team camps, we would get to know hundreds of coaches from all over the country. They got to learn about our philosophy and the culture of Tiger Style, which helped elevate our recruiting. All of this took an enormous amount of time and effort, but looking back, it was a fun experience that helped elevate our program.

When I talk about this to people today, I emphasize the process. You start with a vision, then you dive into the hard work necessary to make it happen. If you approach it positively, it can be a rewarding time in your life. Even now, as we aim for the national title, it's a process, but it's always fun. We've kept improving and made great things happen through hard work and a positive mindset.

IT JUST DOESN'T MATTER

In the movie *Meatballs*, Bill Murray plays a character named Tripper, who gives a powerful (and amusing) speech to the kids at Camp North Star. The camp is made up of less wealthy kids who are competing against the more affluent and better-equipped Camp Mohawk. Each summer, the two camps face off in an olympiad with various events like swimming, wrestling, and running. However, Camp North Star has lost to Camp Mohawk for twelve years in a row, which has instilled a defeatist attitude in the North Star campers.

After a particularly rough first day of competition, where Camp North Star gets pummeled and bullied by the arrogant

Mohawk campers (who are also cheaters), the morale at North Star is at an all-time low. That night, Tripper steps up to give the kids a pep talk. He acknowledges that Camp Mohawk has better athletes, superior facilities, and more money. Yet he leads the campers in a chant, proclaiming, "It just doesn't matter!"

Tripper's message is that all the advantages of Camp Mohawk don't matter. What matters is that the kids at Camp North Star go out there, have fun, and give their best effort. As Tripper and the campers continue the chant, "It just doesn't matter," they start to laugh and bond, and a new positive attitude is born.

The next day, inspired by their new mindset, the campers of North Star compete with renewed vigor and spirit. They begin winning events and ultimately pull off an unexpected upset against Camp Mohawk. It's a classic underdog story with a humorous and heartfelt twist, thanks in large part to Bill Murray's speech (which the actor reportedly ad-libbed during filming).

This scene from *Meatballs* has become an inspirational reference for our program, including myself. We even use the quote, "That's just the attitude we *do* need," within our team. Whenever someone goes above and beyond, like staying after practice for an extra session, or an academic advisor giving up their personal time to help, or our trainer coming in on an off day to treat our injured wrestlers, we acknowledge it with that phrase. This approach has helped us create a positive environment by constantly emphasizing the importance of a good attitude.

Tripper's speech reminds us that focusing on what we have and maintaining a positive outlook can drive us to success, even against seemingly impossible odds.

OUR WEEKLY MEETINGS

People often ask me about our weekly team meetings and how they help keep everyone focused on what we have rather than what others have. This question comes up frequently during my talks. The truth is, our weekly meetings play a fundamental role in maintaining focus and guiding behavior.

Our meetings are actually twofold: a weekly staff meeting and our Mental Monday sessions with the team. Both are designed to align our staff and team so that everyone is on the same page for the week. They also give us a great opportunity every week to foster our Tiger Style culture.

Staff meetings begin with academics, which is a core part of our identity at the University of Missouri. Students come here primarily for their education, and wrestling is an additional pursuit. So, we start with updates from our academic advisor. We discuss who is attending classes and who might be struggling, and we address any concerns. Then we move on to other areas like compliance, sports information, marketing, and input from our strength coach and trainer.

I encourage input from everyone at these meetings. It's important for staff members to feel valued and heard, which in turn boosts their morale and commitment. When people feel like their contributions matter, they become more willing to give their best effort. I always remember Teddy Roosevelt's quote: "People don't care how much you know until they know how much you care." This philosophy is central to all of our meetings.

Mental Monday sessions involve both the coaching staff and the team. Each week, we focus on a different topic, such as motivation, identity, or tournament preparation. We start with a large-group discussion, where I lead but also ask many questions to engage the team. Then we break into smaller groups guided by assistant coaches. This setup makes it easier for everyone to share and participate, which promotes a collaborative environment. These sessions are instrumental in setting the right mindset for the week, while also addressing any areas where we need improvement.

At the end of each season, we also conduct year-end reviews. I send out questions to the entire staff, asking for their feedback on what they did well, areas for improvement, and suggestions for the team and program to improve. This process includes everyone from academic advisors to marketing staff. We compile all of these insights to create a plan of action for the next year. This collective input helps us improve in areas like fan engagement, injury prevention, and performance in the weight room.

Additionally, I meet with athletes individually, along with another coach who works closely with them. We discuss what they did well, areas for improvement, and how they can contribute even more to the team. We also identify who has positively impacted them during the season. This feedback helps us recognize and encourage those who are making a difference and allows us to put together personalized plans for each athlete's development.

This year, I introduced new weekly sessions with Ben Loeb, an accomplished high school tennis coach and mental performance consultant. His book *Next-Level Coaching* has provided valuable insights for our Mental Monday sessions. Ben now works with our coaching staff to enhance our mental coaching skills. This collaboration has been incredibly beneficial, and it has given our coaches more ideas, preparing them better for mental training sessions. And our athletes have greatly benefited from these enhanced mental coaching strategies.

All of these meetings, from the weekly staff meetings and Mental Monday sessions to year-end reviews, play a vital role in keeping our team focused on what we have. By involving everyone, encouraging input, and continually seeking improvement, we are building a stronger and more unified culture. This approach not only creates a positive environment but also drives our team to achieve their best.

EXERCISE 1: *IT JUST DOESN'T MATTER*

One exercise I like to do with my team involves watching a scene from the movie *Meatballs*. At the time of this writing, you can find the scene on YouTube: "It Just Doesn't Matter."[1] After we watch the video, I ask my team members what they learned from it.

I also like to show this video clip when I give talks to other groups. It's amusing to watch the reactions of businesspeople when I show them the clip. Initially, they're usually puzzled and wonder, "What the hell are we watching?" But soon enough, they start laughing, and the atmosphere lightens up. Afterward, we discuss the lessons from the pep talk.

The central theme, of course, is to not compare ourselves with others. In the movie, the characters were comparing themselves to their wealthier, better-equipped rivals. They focused on what the other camp had rather than what they themselves could achieve. I will ask the group, "Do you have people in your business who exhibit this attitude? How can we change this mindset?"

For my team, I encourage them to focus on the good within our own program. What do we have? We have people who

1   "It Just Doesn't Matter! - Meatballs (6/9) Movie CLIP (1979) HD," YouTube video, posted November 22, 2011, *https://www.youtube.com/ watch?v=-TogGxzlfhM*

do great things and are motivated. Find the positives in your program. The characters in the movie were also focused on the outcome rather than the process and the joy of competition. Once they started to embrace the competition and enjoy the process, they began to succeed and have fun.

This scene and its message serve as a reminder that there must be some fun involved in what we do. As part of the group discussion, talk about how you can create enjoyment in your work and foster a positive attitude.

EXERCISE 2: **PRACTICING GRATITUDE**

I have another exercise I like to do with my team where I ask them to tell me five things they're grateful for. I started to notice more mental health struggles among young people in the years after the pandemic. So many young people these days feel like things aren't going well, their outlook is bleak, and they focus on the negative. I address this with my team by encouraging them to think about the positive aspects of their day. Sometimes they'll say they can't think of anything positive, and that's when I remind them of the little things.

For example, I'll say, "Did you eat at the athletic dining hall today?" And when they say, "Yes," I point out how amazing the food is there and how fortunate they are to have great team-mates to share the meal with. It's remarkable how their attitude starts to shift once they begin to recognize the good things in their lives. They'll start mentioning other positives, like doing well in a class or having supportive friends.

Every Friday, we have a tradition called Grateful Friday. We gather as a team on the mat and form a circle. Each person has the opportunity to step into the circle and express gratitude. It's not mandatory, but usually about six or seven people choose to participate. They'll thank someone for helping them with a technique, tutoring them in a difficult subject, or simply being there to lift their spirits when they are feeling down.

This practice helps us reinforce the attitude we want to cultivate within our team—the attitude of gratitude. It's a wonderful way to wrap up the workweek on a positive note.

CHAPTER 4

BELIEVE AND FIND A WAY

NEVER PLANNED TO become a wrestler. Growing up, I played basketball, lacrosse, and football. Wrestling wasn't even on my radar. But one weekend after football season ended, my father took me for a drive and asked me what I planned to play next. Without hesitation, I told him. "I'm going to try out for basketball!"

What he said next caught me off guard.

"Basketball? Have you looked at our family? We're not very tall. I'm not saying you can't make the basketball team—you've always been successful. But wrestling would be good for football."

Up to that point, I had never considered wrestling, but when my father told me it would improve my football performance, it piqued my interest. So, I joined the team and started wrestling in ninth grade. That's a late start compared to most successful wrestlers, and to be honest, at first I wasn't fully committed to it. Wrestling was just something to do between seasons that would help me stay in shape.

It wasn't until my sophomore year, when I made it to the state championships and almost beat the second- and third-place finishers, that I saw my potential. At that point, I thought to myself, "If I ever got serious about this sport, I might be pretty good."

Around this time, my cousin Kevin, a successful high school wrestling coach, reached out to me. He invited me to come to New York to work for his landscaping business over the summer and train in wrestling. I took him up on the offer. Those seven weeks with him changed everything. They transformed my approach to wrestling and, in many ways, my approach to life. From that moment on, wrestling became my central focus.

Returning home, I faced a tough conversation with my father—I had decided to give up football. I worried he would be disappointed. But, in the true fashion of my amazing parents, he was nothing but supportive.

"Go find a way to become the best wrestler you can be," he told me.

My parents had always encouraged us to pursue our passions, whatever they might be, and his approval gave me the confidence I needed to go for it.

By the time I was eighteen, wrestling had consumed my life. Every day, I woke up thinking about what I could do to improve. This dedication has remained unwavering. Now, at fifty-eight, I look back on forty years of living and breathing wrestling (and coaching wrestling). It has helped shape my identity, driven my journey, and fueled my pursuit of excellence. Wrestling has provided me with a platform that allows me to share Tiger Style, which is the essence of who I am.

TODD'S REDEMPTION STORY

Todd Schavrien was a very successful wrestler who almost walked away from success. We were preparing for a dual meet at home against Nebraska. About an hour before the weigh-ins, I couldn't find Todd anywhere. When I started asking other people if they'd seen him, everyone seemed to avoid the question. Finally, someone admitted, "I think Todd is driving home."

I was stunned. "Driving home? Todd's from California, and we're in Missouri," I said.

As it turned out, Todd was indeed on his way home. He'd gotten discouraged before the meet, and convinced he would miss weight, he'd decided to leave. I quickly got another wrestler ready to make weight for the dual and called Todd. By the time I reached him, he was just outside of Kansas City, which is about two hours from the Hearnes Center. I urged him to pull over and convinced him he couldn't just run away from his problems. It took some effort, but I eventually persuaded him to turn around and come back.

Todd didn't make it back in time for the dual, and we ended up losing because of that weight class. The team was understandably furious with him. On Monday, I met with the team and informed them that I had convinced Todd to return. I asked how they felt about it, and the response was unanimous: No one wanted him back.

Despite their feelings, I decided to give Todd another chance. I started by having him practice separately from the team and involved him with a different group of people. Gradually, I integrated him back into the team, first working out with him myself and then allowing him to practice with his teammates. Over time, the team began to accept him again.

By the end of the season, Todd helped us perform well at the conference and became a national qualifier. His mindset and attitude improved, and he started to be accepted by his teammates. He not only turned things around but also was voted team captain. He went on to become a Big 12 champion and an All-American.

Here is Todd's side of the story:

TODD'S STORY: *TURNING THE CAR AROUND*

It all started about five or six hours before our home dual against Nebraska. We were three-quarters of the way through the season, and I had a losing record and zero home wins. I had about two pounds left to lose, and I wasn't particularly enthusiastic about doing so just to finish out the season .500 at best. That being the case, I decided I would take the easy way out and sauna the weight off. Only, when I got out of the sauna, I was still 1.6 pounds over. I had some time before the dual, but only losing 0.4 pounds completely broke me and opened the floodgates of negative thoughts.

I decided to call it quits. I went back to my place, packed a bag, and started driving to California. I didn't tell my coaches because I knew there was still a manageable amount of time to lose the weight, and they would convince me to do so. But I was done. I didn't want to make weight that day or ever again; I just wanted to quit.

Looking back now, I believe I must have known subconsciously I didn't really want to quit because I had already planned a stop only two and a half hours into the trip to visit a friend of mine who played baseball at the University of Kansas. I should mention that at this time in my life, I viewed almost everything as transactional. My view of the athlete/coach relationship, for example, was that I was the talent and his job rested on my abilities. There was only one twenty-five-pounder and one other thirty-three-pounder besides me, and he was a true freshman and, frankly, not all that great. So, I assumed if I had a change of heart and wanted to come back, the coaches would have no choice but to take me back.

I turned off my phone and started driving. About an hour into the drive, I turned my phone back on, and I had several missed calls from one particular coach. Shortly afterward, I got a call from another coach. I knew I was far enough at this point that they couldn't make me come back and make weight, so I answered.

The coach asked me if I was coming to the dual, and I said no. He expressed his disappointment, and that was the extent of the conversation. Then, a little later, I got a call from Coach Smith. He told me to pull over so we could talk. I did, and he asked me to turn around and come back. He told me I would not need to come to the dual or practice the next day. He said I could take the weekend to think about whether I wanted to come back or not, and we would meet on Monday.

I pulled off at the next exit, went through a KFC drive-through, ordered a ridiculous amount of food, and started driving back to Columbia. I remember finishing the food and feeling extremely unsatisfied. I had a full belly, and it wasn't as great as I had made it out to be while cutting weight. I knew that on Monday I was going to tell Coach Smith I wanted to come back.

My team ended up losing the dual by one point. They pulled a freshman's redshirt, and he got majored by a kid I ended up beating later that year at the Big 12 championships. So, it's very easy to make the argument that the team would have won the dual if I'd been there.

On Monday, I walked into Coach Smith's office to apologize and tell him I wanted to come back and finish out the season. He responded by telling me that the team had taken a vote, and they didn't want me back. This gutted me on so many levels, but it was the moment when it first hit me: I was part of a team, and my actions actually affected other people.

Coach then told me that he had voted for me to stay, and his vote would be the only one that mattered. Still, he imposed a few terms that I would have to agree to before I could return: (1) I had to apologize to the team and start being nicer to the trainer; (2) I would have to take part in practices separate from the team until I could prove I was ready to be part of the team; and (3) when I got back on the team, I would be a backup.

The freshman who took my place at the dual would be the starter from now on, but at some point, there might be an opportunity for me to challenge for the spot. That meant I would have to win two consecutive matches to become the starter, and the freshman would only have to win one to retain the spot. It was certainly not how I expected the conversation to go, but I begrudgingly accepted the terms.

It was quiet for a little bit, then Coach Smith said something I will never forget because it completely altered how I viewed the situation. He said, "Give me a banquet story." Before he said that, I was mad that I wasn't back in the starting lineup, let alone back on the team at all. But the moment he said that, I almost magically started viewing everything as a process, with the end result being one hell of a story to tell at the end-of-year banquet my senior year.

Coach Smith left me in his office to collect my thoughts before I apologized to the team. He went and met with them, explained what my path back would look like, and prepared them for me to apologize. I don't remember much about the apology itself. I recall feeling like no one believed or accepted anything I said. I didn't blame them; I knew actions spoke louder than words.

I also remember going to my locker after giving the apology and discovering that all my gear was gone. This was a common practice when someone quit the team. Guys on the team would take their clothes because it's an honor to wear that gear around campus, and the quitter had lost the right to do so. I had just told everyone I quit a few days earlier, so once again, I didn't really blame them for emptying my locker. It was, however, a tangible representation of where I stood with the team that gave me a feeling of isolation and a generally low view of my own importance. That may seem like a bad thing, but in hindsight, it was exactly what I needed in order to get out of my own way.

One guy called me after the apology and expressed his appreciation and acknowledged how difficult it must have been. In return, I told him if he needed a dummy partner for cutting weight or any other mundane tasks, I would be happy to help. He took me up on the offer, as did other guys over time. At the time, I made the offer just to feel relevant again, be around the team, and add some level of value. However, I was so grateful for them to acknowledge me that I was more than willing to do whatever they needed. For the first time since moving to Missouri, I had a vested interest in someone other than myself.

In a roundabout way, I benefitted and grew from this experience. I learned that we are created for community, fashioned for fellowship, and formed for family, and none of us can fulfill God's purpose by ourselves.

It was during the period of time when I was trying to earn my way back on the team that I was introduced to the first pillar of Tiger Style: the power of Belief. I participated in individual practices with Coach Smith and quickly realized through the time and effort he invested in me that this was not a transactional relationship for him. That was all I needed to know to establish trust and belief in his process, which is where long-lasting, sustainable change started to happen for me.

Once I stopped questioning my coaches, every action and direction ceased to be a burden for me. I also realized why Coach Smith had told me to be nicer to the trainer. My constant questioning of people who were trying to help me accomplish my goals was not only rude but also counterproductive. I was mentally trying to take on the roles of coach, trainer, and athlete. That's a lot of hats to wear, and it's sure to exhaust anyone to the point of wanting to quit.

When I eventually earned my way back on the team, I was introduced to the second pillar of Tiger Style: Compete. I was now the backup thirty-three-pounder, which meant I got to travel with the team, but the starter would be the one who wrestled. I was just there to carry the scale and step up if he got hurt. Truthfully, I was probably just there so Coach Smith could keep an eye on me while he was out of town. This is where I truly felt like I was on the outside looking in. However, it allowed me to step back and take inventory of the team and the people on it. I paid attention to the guys who were performing at a high level and took note of how they competed, the choices they made, how they handled failure, and so on.

It was clear that they applied a certain approach not only in the wrestling room but also in school and life. The Tiger Style philosophy shaped their attitude, actions, and results.

When I realized this, I became enamored by it, and from that moment on, I made a concerted effort to surround myself with people who embodied this philosophy.

For the remainder of my career, I honed what this experience taught me about the first two pillars of Tiger Style and set out to learn and embody the other two (One More and Expect to Win). I went on to write a fairly decent banquet story, but the impact of this experience, the team culture, and my decision to choose Tiger Style are my North Star whenever I find myself off course these days.

The decision to turn my car around that day changed my life forever. It led to me being back on the team, becoming an All-American, getting two degrees, making lifetime friendships, discovering Christ, and even meeting my wife.

—Todd Schavrien

I often think about the impact of my decision to make Todd turn his car around. It changed his life trajectory. He graduated, coached with me, earned his master's in business, and became one of the program's greats. Today, he's a successful business-man with a family.

During that challenging period, Todd found faith as well, which became a cornerstone of his life. Our Fellowship of Christian Athletes (FCA) huddle, a long-standing tradition where team members meet weekly, played a significant role in his transformation. Influential figures like Michael Chandler, Mark Ellis, and Raymond Jordan, who were also part of the FCA, helped him navigate his struggles and grow.

Todd's story reminds me of the importance of persever-ance, community, and personal growth, and it underscores the incredible potential for transformation when someone is given a second chance to find their way.

THE "FIND A WAY" ATTITUDE

Although it's not one of our four pillars, the "Find a Way" attitude is pivotal to our Tiger Style culture. Often, people fixate on their limitations, and in doing so, they give up. Like Todd's initial decision, they assume there's no way forward, so they run away. Todd had no idea how much he was driving away from that day—not just one dual meet but a whole lifetime of opportunities that lay before him. Fortunately, he made the wise decision to come back, to believe in himself, to keep trying, to find a way, and it made all the difference.

But why did he decide to come back? What enabled him to turn the car around? A change in vision. He went from feeling hopeless to seeing a way forward. It was a vision of what could be that brought him back.

A vision of what could be is what drove me during my early days in the old wrestling room. We had the worst facilities on campus, but instead of lamenting, we took action to make it better—to find a way. Sometimes, as I said, that meant grabbing a bucket of paint and transforming the space ourselves. Over time, our efforts paid off, and we created a space that we felt good about.

When the university decided to build a new arena, I had a vision of turning the old practice gym into our new wrestling room. I approached a graphics professor and asked him to create a poster depicting the basketball practice gym as a wrestling room. That poster hung outside my office for two years. Whenever the basketball staff saw it, they were curious. I explained that when the arena was built, I wanted to convert the practice gym into our wrestling room. This vision slowly gained traction. Volleyball and gymnastics teams were also eyeing the gym, but over time, everyone assumed wrestling would claim it.

One day, Mike Alden, head of Missouri athletics, approached me and asked if the gym would suffice as a better facility. I assured him it would be a championship facility. The vision on that poster became a reality.

Through a clear vision and determination, what seems impossible can be achieved. This approach extends beyond physical spaces, of course. For example, the book you're reading right now was originally a vision I had. It was a goal I set for myself, and I shared the goal publicly to hold myself accountable. People started anticipating the book, they encouraged me to follow through on my vision, and their anticipation propelled me forward.

In a similar way, my daughter always had a lot of places around the world that she wanted to visit, so she created a Pinterest board filled with images and links to all these exotic locations. Now, as she has the opportunity to visit these places, she is realizing her dreams. Her Pinterest board served as a visual representation of her goals, constantly reminding her to pursue them, and that vision has driven her to achieve those goals. Her board has those same pictures on it with one addition: She is in them.

In all three cases—for Todd, for me, for my daughter—visualizing goals turned dreams into reality. So many people suppress their aspirations because they fear their goals are unattainable. However, by clarifying a vision, expressing our dreams, and making them tangible, they become achievable. That's what the Find a Way attitude is all about. Create a vision, believe in it, make it known, and relentlessly pursue it until it becomes a reality.

LEADERSHIP IN ACTION

Mike Alden's leadership in Missouri athletics exemplified the Find a Way attitude. For seventeen years of my coaching career, he served as a remarkable athletic director. Mike had a unique ability to inspire people to follow him with his actions, not just his words.

He arrived at the university three months after I was hired. From the beginning, his approach to leadership was hands-on and deeply involved. There were instances before football season when the campus needed urgent attention. Budget constraints meant tasks like picking up garbage or trimming trees were often hard to get to. But instead of delegating these tasks, Mike took matters into his own hands. Many times, I would see him out there with a chainsaw, cutting down tree branches or picking up trash. Watching our top leader do these kinds of physical tasks motivated others to join in.

This approach reminded me of the concept called "sweep the sheds," from James Kerr's book *Legacy*, which describes the culture of the New Zealand All Blacks rugby team. According to Kerr, before leaving the locker room at the end of a game, the senior team members would clean and tidy the room themselves. This mentality has helped to create a culture of humility and collective responsibility among the All Blacks. Mike embodied this same mentality at Missouri, and it profoundly influenced me and many others. Many of Mike's associate ADs are now athletic directors at many Division 1 universities across the country (Alden's Army).

In our wrestling program, we also adopted Mike's approach. Managers will often help clean the practice room, and when they aren't available, instead of merely ordering the team to do it, I often take the initiative myself. I'll gladly grab a mop or a sprayer and go to work. Why do we do this? Because the room needs to be cleaned, and we have the opportunity to do it.

Finding a way is about doing what needs to be done, in humility, to achieve your vision—in this case, a vision of maintaining and caring for our beautiful championship facilities. Usually, when athletes see me doing this kind of work, they quickly offer to take over. It's leadership by example, which we need so desperately in the world. In sports, in business, in politics, and in life, we need leaders who are on the front lines, doing what needs to be done—finding a way—because it inspires others to follow suit.

OVERCOMING FEAR AND TAKING RISKS

Why do people sometimes give up on their dreams, hopes, and aspirations? Why do they see the challenges before them— whether it's a tough dual meet, budget constraints, or seemingly impossible odds—and run the other way instead of finding a way?

I think it's usually due to fear—either a fear of failure or a fear of what others might think. People worry about the consequences of trying and failing to achieve their goals, and they convince themselves that not trying is the better, safer, less embarrassing option. For example, what if I had put up the picture of the new wrestling room, but then they gave it to some other team? That would have been potentially embarrassing for me.

That fear of failure—of being embarrassed at not achieving your stated goal or realizing your dream—can be paralyzing. Nobody wants to be seen as a failure. Often, they would just rather not stick their neck out in the first place.

In athletics, this fear is prevalent. Athletes might dream of becoming state champions, but the thought of the hard work required, and the uncertainty of success, can deter them. Instead of committing fully and risking failure, they doubt their capabilities from the outset. They say, "I don't know if I'm good enough," and use that uncertainty as an excuse to not put in the effort.

Often, the biggest challenge a person faces is overcoming fear and being willing to take risks regardless of potential failure. To do that, you have to adopt a mindset that says, "I don't know if I'm good enough, but I'm going to give it my all, no matter what happens." This attitude—embracing the fear and pushing through it—distinguishes those who find a way to succeed from those who give up (and miss out).

When I first started coaching at Mizzou, as I've said, we didn't have much of a fan base because, quite frankly, no one really believed in us yet. To get people to our matches, we began by inviting our neighbors, offering tickets to people at church, and reaching out to friends, parents, and children. We found a spot in the Hearnes Center where we could host indoor tailgates, which turned our wrestling events into social gatherings. This initiative helped us attract more fans, and word spread that our matches were both fun and competitive.

But the point is, we had to believe in ourselves and commit to giving our all long before anyone noticed or cared about what we were doing. That's why the *first* pillar of Tiger Style is Believe. Over time, as our team improved, our fan base grew, and other people began to believe in us too.

Wrestling offers fans a unique closeness to the athletes since spectators can sit right beside the mat. We started selling these prime seats for $300 to $400 a season, and they quickly sold out. By creating a lively and engaging experience, we eventually managed an average of over 3,000 spectators per match, with some events drawing nearly 7,000 fans. Our success at growing a fan base was partly due to the matches themselves, but largely due to the social experience we cultivated around them.

It all started because we committed to making this wrestling program successful before anyone else had confidence we could do it. And that right there is my advice to coaches and business leaders alike: There is always a way, so *believe*.

If you can't attract people to your events or sell your product, don't give up or walk away in defeat and embarrassment. Be confident in your team, your business, your product, and yourself, and give it your all. You might need to rethink your approach, as we did. Take inspiration from Apple, which sells a lifestyle rather than just a product. We've done something similar with our Tiger Style brand, promoting it as a lifestyle that our athletes embody. They're not just wrestlers. They are smart young people pursuing high-level degrees and actively involved in the community, which makes them relatable and admirable to our fans.

We also engage with local businesses, offering internships to our athletes and inviting these businesses to our events. We created Tigers with Style, a group offering cheaper tickets and special seating for organizations. These groups come for the social outings but often leave as enthusiastic wrestling fans. For example, the head of a local bank, who had never attended a wrestling match in his life, enjoyed the experience so much that he requested mat-side seats in his donation to Missouri Athletics.

Believe! There is always a way!

SELLING SHOES AND RECRUITING TOP TALENT

Often, it's a matter of having the right perspective. Instead of seeing insurmountable obstacles, you see challenging opportunities. It reminds me of a story I once heard. It goes something like this.

A shoe company sent a salesman to a third-world country where people didn't wear shoes. The salesman got there, saw everyone walking around in bare feet, and thought, "This is ridiculous. These people aren't going to buy shoes. They don't *wear* shoes!" He saw it as a lost cause, so he returned home discouraged.

The shoe company decided to try again. They sent a second salesman to the same country. This young man had a different perspective. When he saw all of the people walking around in bare feet, he thought, "Wow, this must be the easiest place in the world to sell shoes because they don't wear shoes!" He saw opportunities where the previous salesman saw only obstacles.

In the end, the second salesman sold a whole lot of shoes. The same situation, viewed differently, led to a vastly different outcome.

This mindset played a big role in recruiting Ben Askren. Ben was an exceptional athlete from Wisconsin. Missouri had yet to achieve national recognition in wrestling, so when I started recruiting him, I sold him on a vision: He could become our first national champion and an Olympian, a legend who would change our program.

Other recruiters warned him against joining us due to our lack of history, but Ben was drawn to the challenge. He saw opportunity, not obstacles.

Ben's personality and work ethic were unique. He admired Muhammad Ali and shared Ali's confidence and charisma. During high school, he used to boast in chat rooms about his wrestling prowess, which made him a polarizing figure. But his confidence was backed by his dedication to training. I knew he could be the Pied Piper for our program, helping us attract others through his success and leadership.

Inspired by the opportunity to make history, Ben committed to wrestle for Missouri. Ultimately, he became our first national champion and led the team to a third-place finish at the NCAAs. His impact was transformative to our entire program, attracting top recruits from all over and further changing our culture. Today, Ben continues to influence the wrestling world through his wrestling academies in Wisconsin, and many of his students choose to wrestle at Mizzou because of their admiration for him.

We'll look at Ben's story a little closer later, and we'll even hear from Ben himself. For now, I just want to say that Ben Askren exemplifies the Find a Way attitude. It's an attitude that looks beyond the obvious and embraces challenges with creativity and determination. Whether that means growing a fan base, leading a team, or recruiting top talent, the key is to see opportunities where others see obstacles and to inspire those around you with a clear vision and a relentless pursuit of success.

EXERCISE 1: GET REGULAR FEEDBACK

Every year, as the season draws to a close, I make it a point to ask every team member and staff member for feedback on how I can improve as head coach. This is just one part of creating an environment where my athletes and staff feel comfortable offering honest suggestions. I encourage them to share their thoughts either through email, in one-on-one meetings, or in larger group settings without fear of offending me.

In addition to seeking feedback on my performance, I also ask each member of my staff to identify one area where they can improve in their own personal development so they are contributing even more to the team's success. For example, some coaches have committed to becoming more organized or improving their recruiting efforts.

I also seek input on changes that would benefit the entire program. Often, the suggestions I get are straightforward yet impactful. One notable example was when my athletes mentioned the lack of a water fountain in the locker room. Installing a water fountain was a simple fix, but it significantly boosted their morale and demonstrated my investment in their well-being.

Even feedback from people who are indirectly involved with the team can be invaluable. Our team doctor, for example, has provided valuable insights into recruiting strategies by drawing parallels with how he attracts elite doctors to his orthopedic group. His outsider perspective prompted us to brainstorm new, innovative approaches to attracting top-tier talent. It's all about giving every person in the program a chance to help us collectively find a way toward greater success.

Consulting mentors from various industries also offers fresh perspectives. My brother, who runs one of the largest asphalt companies in the United States, faces similar challenges as me in employee management and organizational development. By discussing these issues with him and others, I gain new ideas for fostering a positive culture and driving success.

EXERCISE 2: *LEADERSHIP REACTION COURSE "PLATE DRILL"*

The following exercise was shared with me by retired Marine Mike Mendoza. This is a great example of leadership and finding a way.

SETUP
1. You will need three cones and five differently weighted plates numbered one to five.

2. The three cones should be spaced in a line at least twenty feet apart. If possible, place the cones on rolling hills so they are not visible to all team members. This forces more communication and leadership.

SITUATION

All plates start at Cone 1 in a stack from heaviest (on the bottom) to lightest (on the top.

MISSION

Stack the plates in the same order at Cone 3 as fast as possible.

COORDINATING INSTRUCTIONS

1. Only one plate can be moved at a time.
2. Only the top plate in the stack can be moved.
3. At no time can a heavier plate be stacked on a lighter plate.
4. Only one stack can be made at each cone.
5. All commands must come from the group leader.
6. If two plates are picked up at one time, or a heavier plate is stacked on a lighter plate, the team must be penalized.
7. Penalty: one minute of exercise and then restart.
8. The team has eight minutes to complete the task.

DEBRIEF

1. The coach should ask the leader what they thought they did well and what they think they need to improve.
2. The opportunity should then be given to the team to evaluate the leader and themselves.
3. The coach should then ask the leader or teammates one thing they learned that they can and will apply to their job/team/school.

4. Upon completion, the coach will first review the standards that great teammates and great leaders consistently meet and exceed. Then they will discuss one of the suggested Learning Objectives below.

LEARNING OBJECTIVES:

1. **The role of team leaders and the role of teammates**: Stress that the leader communicates the plan and then the team starts executing on that plan. If teammates have suggestions after that, they should go to the leader and discuss, but everyone shouting and pitching in their two cents is not helpful. Once a plan has been communicated, your job is to do everything you can to make that plan succeed. Complaining about it is not helpful. You undermine our own team and your own chances of mission success. If it is your turn to be a good team leader, then be a good team leader. If it isn't, then be a good teammate and run the damn plate! This lesson is especially important when the terrain allows the team leader to see the big picture, while some teammates can't see the other cones.

2. **Common sense and control**: You may not always be the genius who comes up with the plan, but you will still be held accountable for the result and need to control your team.

CHAPTER 5

COMPETE

SOME YEARS AGO, my assistants and I wanted to find a better way to recruit effectively, so we sat down and devised a checklist of important attributes to look for in recruits. We analyzed past recruits and identified traits that led to their success, and those traits formed the basis of our checklist. One of the most important traits, we realized, was a natural drive to compete.

So now, I focus on recruiting people who compete in everything they do. I want wrestlers who are competitors by nature, always striving to do better, be better, and succeed. Indeed, Compete is one of the core values of Tiger Style (Believe, Compete, One More, Expect to Win).

For the most part, recruiting top-tier wrestlers is pretty straightforward (though not always easy) because you know where to look for the best athletes: national tournaments. In other sports, in other fields, and in business, identifying the top performers in the field may be a bit more complicated and involve a lot of different criteria. However, I believe certain principles remain the same across the board.

A competitive drive to always get better is a trait that makes a good wrestler, a good basketball player, a good salesman, a good teacher, a good farmer, and just about anything else. It's a universally beneficial trait. I also prioritize intelligence and work ethic, which I gauge through GPAs. A recruit's desire to excel, not just in sports but in class, including subjects they struggle with or just don't enjoy, is key. If a student works hard in a challenging class, it shows their commitment to self-improvement, which will benefit them in every area of their lives, including on the mat. We also value recruits who have goals beyond wrestling because we aim to develop well-rounded individuals.

I appreciate people who love to compete and get better in everything. Whether it's a custodian finding ways to improve cleanliness or an equipment manager finding better ways to organize, they demonstrate a commitment to excellence in whatever they do.

Competing means facing adversity and putting yourself on the line, not just winning, and true competition involves continual effort, determination, and resilience. This philosophy is central to our Tiger Style culture. Even through setbacks, we are committed to growing and improving. There will never be a perfect practice or competition, but having the mindset to always strive to learn and improve is what ultimately makes us better.

A certain story about Tiger Woods has always stuck with me. He was working with his golf coach on a new swing, and during the learning phase, his scores initially worsened. Someone watching him without understanding what was going on might have assumed that he was getting worse at the game. However, as he continued to practice the new swing, his scores began to improve.

Eventually, he surpassed his previous performance and began playing better than ever. In a sense, he had to take a step back in order to make progress and get better. But when you're constantly competing, always striving to get better, these are the short-term setbacks you're willing to accept in order to achieve more. If Tiger Woods hadn't been striving to get better, if he'd been willing to settle, then he wouldn't have made the short-term sacrifice to learn a new swing.

I look for this same quality in recruits. Good recruits don't settle for their current level of performance. They're always seeking ways to improve, to challenge themselves, to find a better way.

GETTING BETTER TOGETHER

A competitor also needs to be a great teammate. Wrestling is not a one-man show, even though it may seem that way. As part of a team, every wrestler must strive to help the *whole* team, to elevate everyone else, not just themselves. Otherwise, the best wrestler in the world can become detrimental to team performance.

I always ask recruits about their team and their role within that team. I listen for enthusiasm in their responses, especially when they express enjoyment in helping teammates improve. This collaborative spirit is vital to success. Competition without a collaborative spirit is destructive. The two must go hand in hand.

That's as true in sports as it is in business. Success comes from driven individuals who are willing to work together and support one another. I recall Keegan O'Toole, a two-time national champion. During his senior year in high school, he was more excited about his teammates' success than his own.

I witnessed this at the semifinal round of his state tournament where he was competing for his fourth state title. He was pinning his opponent but was watching another match. The ref kept trying to raise his hand after he won, but he pulled away to run and watch his teammate win an upset in the semifinal round. That kind of selflessness and team spirit are intangible qualities that elevate an entire program.

I model this for my team by collaborating with other coaches, sharing insights about our culture and recruiting strategies. I'm not just trying to make Missouri wrestling the best athletics program on campus. I'm also fostering a community of shared growth and support with other programs. I want to lift up our program, but I want to elevate all of Missouri athletics as well.

Similarly, another quality I look for when recruiting is respectfulness toward family and coaches. A recruit who respects their family and coaches is likely to be respectful within our community.

A great teammate values collaboration and problem-solving because they have a growth mindset that continually seeks improvement. After a tough practice, instead of walking away feeling defeated, they stay to work on their weaknesses. Just like in the business world, a salesperson with a growth mindset might have a day when they don't close any deals. Instead of walking away defeated, they spend some time practicing and refining their sales pitches. This kind of self-driven effort is absolutely vital.

I had my own growth experience not long after becoming head coach at Missouri. I was asked to give a speech to 400 high school wrestling coaches. I had very little experience with public speaking at that point, but I did my best. I thought my speech went well, but afterward, the emcee came up to me and handed me a book on public speaking. I got the hint. I needed to improve!

Instead of walking away feeling dejected, I took his recommendation to heart and began studying public speaking techniques and analyzing speeches to become a better communicator. That's a growth mindset.

During our recruitment process, we emphasize Tiger Style and engage in discussions to see if a recruit resonates with our culture. If they show genuine interest and enthusiasm, it's a good sign they will fit in well. We want recruits who truly want to be part of our program. If two recruits are similar in almost every way, I will choose the one who has shown a stronger desire to join us. This dedication is an invaluable quality.

Attributes like these go beyond physical skills. They contribute significantly to the team's success and cohesion. Ultimately, it's about creating a culture where everyone strives to be their best, supports one another, and continually seeks improvement. Whether in sports or business, this is the kind of attitude that creates successful individuals and a cohesive team.

BUILDING RELATIONSHIPS

Leaders play a key role in turning a competitive spirit into a collaborative environment by developing strong relationships with recruits. One of the most effective methods we've found to do this is through personal notes. While phone calls and texts are common today, a handwritten note can have a more significant impact. It may seem like a small thing, but it's a nostalgic gesture that many kids love. It's unusual and meaningful to receive an actual handwritten letter in their mailbox.

We've created about forty different graphics featuring pictures and quotes related to our Tiger Style culture. Each handwritten note will have one of these graphics on the front, with a personal note from a coach on the back that ties into that week's phone call topic. For example, if the graphic is about "Believe," the note will discuss the importance of believing in something to drive success, which we then elaborate on during the phone call.

This approach has resonated deeply with recruits. Dom Bradley, a former recruit from around 2010 and current assistant coach, still has a stack of notes I sent him. He has saved them for all of these years.

It's a small, personal gesture that shows recruits we care about them and are willing to invest time in them. This personal touch extends beyond recruiting. I send similar notes to donors. This approach is often overlooked in sports *and* business. One of my pet peeves about sales is the lack of follow-up after a sale is made. It feels insincere and transactional when a salesperson disappears as soon as the purchase is completed.

Personally, I work hard to maintain relationships with recruits and their families even after they join the team. I follow up with thank-you notes after visits, keep in touch with parents, and send emails updating them on their wrestler's progress. This continuous engagement builds strong, long-term relationships that continue after our students have graduated and moved on. We have former team members visit us from time to time, and our alumni events, like the one that drew 110 attendees last year, highlight the positive experiences and lasting connections we've built.

Consistent follow-up is key. Whether through phone calls, personal notes, or emails, maintaining a connection shows genuine care. For example, when I was selling lockers as a fundraiser for our upgraded locker room, it wasn't just about making a sale. It was the culmination of regular updates, personal calls, and occasional notes that built trust and rapport. I keep a list of donors and call them just to express gratitude. These calls aren't always about asking for something. Often, they're just to update donors on the team's progress and thank them for their support. Because of these relationships and donors believing in our culture, I was able to get all forty-two lockers sold in nine days.

When you take the time to build relationships, you create a network of people who feel connected and appreciated. In turn, people become more willing to support you because they value the relationship. This principle of relationship building is integral to our program and a significant part of what makes our Tiger Style culture successful.

COMPETITION AND CAMARADERIE

In our program, the word "compete" holds a special significance. When you walk into our training room, you'll immediately see our All-American board, the Academic All-American board, pictures of our national champions, top-ten team rankings, and conference championship teams. I display these boards to our athletes to remind them of what they are striving for.

At the end of each practice, we often engage in competitive drills. These usually involve a mental and physical challenge, such as seeing how many takedowns they can get in four minutes or splitting the team for a takedown tournament. We have three full circles for competition, and I'll tell them to grab a partner and compete in front of everyone, with teammates cheering each other on. This promotes a competitive spirit *and* camaraderie—that incredibly important combination.

For conditioning, we run sprints and shuttle runs. The athletes keep journals to track their times, competing against themselves to improve week by week. This spirit of competition extends beyond physical training. We compete academically as well, with team members striving to get on the Academic All-American board. This commitment to excellence in all areas is why we require our wrestlers to attend every class and use tutors when necessary.

Our competitive spirit even extends to activities like kickball before practice. The intensity of these kickball games is so high that we've had more injuries from kickball than from wrestling because our athletes want to win so badly. If I see someone figuring out strategies to win in a simple game like kickball, I know they'll bring that same determination to the mat.

This combination of a competitive spirit and camaraderie becomes particularly important when a wrestler faces a setback. Drake Houdashelt was the number one seed going into his junior NCAA tournament, but he tore his hamstring in the quarterfinals. He responded to this injury by vowing to do all the little things right and even joked at the 2023 Mizzou Athletic Hall of Fame induction that he literally did everything Coach told him to do to become a national champion. My assistant coach, Todd Schavrien, and our team doctor, Bus Tarbox, decided to text him every day the entire season with the message, "You will be an NCAA champion."

This daily encouragement went on for over 300 days until the morning of the NCAA finals, where Drake ultimately won the national title. This consistent support showed him that we believed in him and helped him stay focused on his goal.

Then there's the story of Jacob Bohlken, a former heavyweight wrestler who was struggling in medical school. He was far from home, his teammates, and his family. We had a funny picture of him with his heavyweight teammates acting as my bodyguards. When my wife and I heard he was having a tough time, we sent him a card with that picture and a message of encouragement. Later, he told me that small gesture meant a lot to him during this difficult period of time.

Effective coaches, just like effective business leaders, remember that people go through tough times and use simple acts of support to lift them up. Sometimes, that's as simple as starting a meeting with recognizing those who are excelling or, as we say it, "living Tiger Style." This positivity and recognition encourages everyone to continue competing at their highest level.

MICHAEL CHANDLER, THE WALK-ON SUPERSTAR

Michael Chandler attended our Tiger Style camps for three summers, and I always noticed the Missouri native's enthusiasm and drive. He frequently expressed his desire to attend the University of Missouri. Despite our interest in him, Michael had never won a state championship, which is a key factor we consider when recruiting.

Going into his senior year, we continued to watch him closely. We admired his tenacity and performance at our camps. During the state tournament, which takes place in our building, I saw Michael compete in the finals. Unfortunately, he lost. Watching him get beaten was a crushing moment because I knew how much he wanted to succeed. However, I had already planned to offer him a walk-on spot, though Michael didn't know this.

After his defeat, he was understandably devastated. Mike Hagerty, another coach in Missouri, found Michael crying in the hallway and tried to console him, encouraging him not to give up on his dream. Michael expressed his fear that losing the state finals meant he had lost his chance to go to Mizzou. Hagerty then called me to share this heartfelt moment. Hearing how much Michael wanted to be part of our team, combined with my admiration for his work ethic, solidified my decision to offer him a walk-on spot.

Today, Michael Chandler has built a brand around his identity as a walk-on. He joined us at the University of Missouri with unmatched determination and grit. During his redshirt year, his fierce competitive spirit caught the attention of many people, including Oklahoma head coach Jack Spates, who called me to praise the middleweight who was making waves.

Michael Chandler was a relentless brawler who never backed down. By his second year, he had earned a starting position on our team and eventually became a scholarship athlete. He qualified for nationals all four years but faced heartbreak, losing in the All-American round twice before his senior year. We all wanted him to break through, and when he finally did, becoming an All-American, it felt like a triumph for the entire team and coaching staff. Michael had transformed from a kid who didn't win the state title to a determined athlete who never gave up on his dream until he achieved it.

After his collegiate wrestling career, Michael decided to pursue a career in the UFC. Initially, people doubted his talent and potential. He seemed to struggle with taking too many punches. Yet, with his unyielding competitive spirit and growth mentality, Michael continued to improve. Today, he is a popular and successful fighter. As I write this book, he is preparing to fight Conor McGregor in what is projected to be the highest-grossing fight in UFC history, having already made $20 million in ticket sales alone before even hitting pay-per-view.

MICHAEL'S STORY: **THE MAN IN MY CORNER**

The year was 2009, and up to that point in my life, nothing had been more important than the All-American round of the NCAA wrestling championships in my hometown of St. Louis, Missouri. It was just over 1,600 days since I first stepped foot on the Mizzou campus as a freshman, and the man I had blossomed into was thanks solely to the man in my corner that day.

I remember waiting in the tunnel at the Scottrade Center—a moment wrestlers in big tournaments know all too well—waiting to be ushered into the battlegrounds. Coach Smith was calm, as he always was—no extra words, no extra hype, just his stoic self. The kind of stoicism that I needed.

I had grown accustomed to the familiar demeanor of the man I respected more than any other in the world. We both knew what was at stake. For me, it was the culmination of five years of doing things the hard way, doing more than what was asked of me, but always falling short in the big moments. As for Coach Smith, he wanted all of his guys to win, but in my particular career, he knew this could be the last match for a kid who had earned the right to be on that All-American podium but hadn't yet found his way.

My opponent was Jonny Bonilla-Bowman from Hofstra University, a guy I had beaten numerous times in the past. As a matter of fact, I had never lost to him. But it was always a tough match, and quite frankly, I hated wrestling the guy. I was more skilled, I was more technical, but he was one of those opponents who would make you work for and earn every single point. I was nervous—maybe the most nervous I had ever been in my entire life up to that point—but isn't that how so many "I almost" stories go? A loss to a guy you had never lost to before.

Our mat was called, and we walked to the mat. I jogged to grab the ankle bands, and we both went to our separate corners for a "last word" with our coaches. Coach Smith's demeanor in that match was no different than it had been for the prior 130 matches, but the look in his eyes was different. He knew what was at stake: an all-or-nothing match in which the loser would go home and the 2009 season—and for me, my entire career—would be over.

"Just go have fun, Michael," he said to me as the referee called us to the center of the mat. He knew that any more words or emphasis at the moment would only do harm and make his athlete, whom he loved, too high on the weight and heaviness of that moment.

I backpedaled slowly, not wanting to unlock my eyes from Coach Smith's. This was one of those moments I want to hang onto forever, and one I will never forget. Maybe it was the fear that this could be our last match together ever, or maybe it was the last little bit of warrior spirit he was instilling in me. The invincibility those eyes could transfer from one man to another was something Coach Smith will never quite understand. For him, he was just doing his job to the best of his ability, but for me and all of his Tigers over the years, he was a cornerstone we all wanted so badly to compete for, to *win* for. Not for the fear of reprimand, but for the fear of underperforming in his program that he had built day in and day out. It meant something to us to wear the black and gold.

But that moment had to end because it was time to go, and the tournament waits for no one.

I'll spare you the details of the match. Ultimately, I won 6-5 in a match in which the score was as much of a battle as who was in control. I finally did it—an NCAA All-American—but more importantly, *we* did it. As my hand was raised, signifying I was the winner of the match, a weight was lifted, but my thoughts went to one thing: I wanted to get off of that mat and share the moment with Coach Smith.

I ran to the corner and jumped into Coach Smith's arms. As much as I am proud that it is my name in the history books of NCAA wrestling, I am immensely prouder that it is my name on the wall at Mizzou and that Coach Smith can take credit for it. I am now married to the woman of my dreams, have two beautiful children, have won multiple world titles in MMA, have built businesses, and have made millions of dollars. I've been all over the world and have experienced highs many humans can only dream of, but that hug on an afternoon in St. Louis, Missouri, was one of the best feelings I have ever felt in my entire life. It was an embrace that was more than a celebration; it was a patrimony and a solidification of all the hard work we had put in for the five years prior.

Coach Smith is as much a father figure as he is a coach; he is as much a mentor as he is an authoritarian. To me, at my age now, over fifteen years removed from college wrestling, he is a friend, but he will forever be a man I admire. I know the competitive blood pumps through my veins because he was once the general who propelled this earthly vessel forward day after day in pursuit of a goal. I am the competitor, husband, father, and man I am today because I was once a Mizzou Tiger, and more specifically, a Mizzou Tiger for Coach Smith.

I am not just an All-American; I am Brian Smith's All-American.

–Michael Chandler

Michael Chandler's journey from a determined walk-on to a celebrated UFC fighter exemplifies the power of resilience, hard work, and unwavering belief in oneself. His story is a testament to the fact that dreams can be achieved through dedication and perseverance. And importantly, he was surrounded by a supportive team and coaches who kept him motivated and encouraged. It's that perfect combination of a competitive spirit and camaraderie, a potent mix that creates champions like nothing else.

CHAPTER 6

THINK RIGHT/SPEAK RIGHT

I N ANY TEAM, whether it's a sports team, a sales team, or some
other kind of group, success largely depends on everyone
being aligned and on the same page. Unity of vision and purpose ensures that everyone is working toward the same goals
and adhering to the same standards, which in turn boosts the
efficiency and effectiveness of the team as a whole. This concept
is vital to our Tiger Style culture, which is designed to foster a
shared belief system that will guide behavior and set a standard
for the actions, thoughts, and communication of every member
of the team.

Tiger Style began with small initiatives that gradually
shaped a culture with a clear set of standards and expectations
for how every wrestler and staff member was to behave and
treat others. And like any culture, our values and beliefs are
reinforced by certain stories that we share regularly with our
team. Much like the stories and parables in the Bible, these
stories we tell and retell offer timeless lessons that demonstrate
our values in action.

In fact, most cultures use the power of storytelling to teach
and reinforce values. It's a powerful and vital part of the human
experience. From the ancient days when tribal elders would sit
in front of the fire and tell stories to our modern age of stream-
ing movies, human culture is built upon stories. In our own
families, we have those stories that we tell and retell. Maybe it's
our grandpa's war experiences or the way our mom and dad first

met. We tell these stories because they remind us of who we are, and they inform the next generation of what matters most to us.

The same goes for whatever culture you are trying to create in your athletic program, team, or business. Whether you're a coach or a business leader, you need to be accumulating stories that will reinforce the values of the culture you're trying to create. I've shared a few of our Tiger Style stories throughout this book. I share these same stories every year.

For example, I like to tell my wrestlers the story of the FedEx driver whose truck broke down in the middle of his route. Determined to continue his deliveries, he wound up hitching a ride with a UPS driver, and lo and behold, he finished his route that day and made all of his deliveries on time. Telling a story like that, and telling it well, resonates a lot more powerfully with team members and employees than a mere platitude, and it reinforces our values of always finding a way and working well with others.

Storytelling is a particularly powerful tool in public speaking because it helps us communicate values and motivate action more effectively than just about anything else. Of course, that requires you to become a good storyteller. As I shared earlier, my first experience with public speaking went so poorly that someone handed me a book on how to become a better public speaker after I stepped away from the podium. However, I received that constructive feedback with humility and went to work improving my speaking ability. I studied powerful speakers, learned from them, and practiced a lot.

Along the way, I learned that powerful public speakers use stories to convey ideas, culture, and beliefs because they are memorable. So I began to work stories into my leadership style, and I saw firsthand how it reinforced our standards. We all know this from experience, even if we don't realize it. When I was a kid, it was a powerful motivator for my parents to tell me, "You'd better behave, or Santa Claus will put coal in your stocking instead of toys!" That was a story that reinforced the standards my parents had set for my behavior.

I don't just tell my wrestlers about Tiger Style values. I share stories about the wrestlers who have come before them, champions who demonstrated a competitive spirit, who showed dedication in every area, both on the mat and in the classroom. In this way, I illustrate each of our principles through storytelling, and the guys get it. The value becomes more than a mere idea; it becomes a concrete action.

For example, as we discussed earlier, one of our core beliefs is One More. I want every team member to commit to doing one more task, making one more effort, because it collectively enhances the team's performance. So, I share stories about people embodying this One More mentality.

If you really want to guide behavior, instill values, and create a cohesive culture within your team or organization, start sharing relatable and memorable stories. Nothing you do as a leader will inspire and motivate your teams, or instill your principles and standards, as powerfully as the stories you tell.

One real-life story I love to tell and retell my wrestlers is about Ben Askren.

UNWAVERING EXPECTATION

Ben Askren always had an unwavering expectation of victory. Even after suffering crushing defeats in his freshman and sophomore years at the NCAA finals, he never lost his confidence. Each loss was devastating, of course. He would retreat, hyperventilating and crying for a long time, unable to speak to the media.

By his junior year, however, Ben was back in the finals. As we rode the bus to the match, I was aware of the high stakes. Missouri had never had a national champion, and Ben was on the verge of either making history or becoming a three-time runner-up. I tried to stay hopeful and positive, but honestly, I was incredibly nervous. Ben, on the other hand, was completely at ease, his personality shining through as he picked out his curly hair into a large afro, laughing and smiling. His carefree demeanor actually started to frustrate me, but he simply reassured me, "Coach, I've got this."

In the tunnel before the match, Ben remained relaxed, looking up at the crowd with a smile. The match was between the two best wrestlers in the country, and only one of them was going to walk away with the Hodge Trophy. But again, Ben told me, "Coach, I've got this."

He dominated that match. His hard work and growth were evident. His mindset was clear. Ben had put in the necessary work, he had learned from his previous losses, and he came there fully prepared. He believed he was going to win, and he did.

I often tell this story to my wrestlers because it illustrates the power of mindset and determination. It's a narrative that resonates and motivates, and it helps me continue to build a successful culture within our team.

Here is Ben's story in his own words:

BEN'S STORY: *THE FIRST NATIONAL CHAMPION*

When I was getting recruited by Missouri in the fall of 2001, a lot of other coaches used the same dig over and over: "They've never had a national champion."

Actually, it was more than just a lot. It was every single one of them. They figured there was no way I'd go to a school that had never produced an NCAA champ (after all, that was my goal), and that was the opening shot they'd fire—in hopes that I'd choose their school instead.

Coach Smith didn't see this as an obstacle. He saw it as an opportunity.

Smart man.

"You can come here and blaze the trail—and put Mizzou on the map," he told me.

Sold!

I had some successes during my redshirt year, such as beating 2003 NCAA champion Rob Waller, but I also struggled at times. I lost to guys who weren't really that good. Instead of berating me, yelling at me, or hitting me when I was down, Coach Smith saw something in me and tried to bring out my best. He saw that not only did I love wrestling, but also I loved tinkering with the process: the techniques and tactics, the moves and mission, what worked and what could work even better.

Coach Smith never dismissed me, and he never tried to shut off my love for experimentation. Instead, it was steady encouragement. He was always there to keep me moving in the right direction.

In the first match of my career—against the number-one-ranked Chris Pendleton—I started out on fire. Using unorthodox techniques, I built a 7-1 lead. But I got over-aggressive, squandered the lead, and lost 9-7 in overtime. While I managed one victory against Chris that year, he was just better than me and beat me in the national finals.

At the start of my sophomore year, I was ranked second and Chris was ranked first. Chris Pendleton was my obstacle. He was the one keeping me from becoming Mizzou's first national champion. I had wrestled him three times, and all three matches were razor close. But I lost them all and failed a second time to become a national champion.

That loss hurt *way* more. Two years in a row losing to the same guy. It stung.

After my last loss, I sat in the back hallway crying and having a really hard time composing myself. When I finished, I resolved that I would not lose in college again—I would do what I had set out to do: become Mizzou's first national champion.

In my junior year, I dominated, going 44-0 with 25 pins. For the national championship, I was facing Jake Herbert, who had been equally dominant. But I knew I had a secret weapon. I watched Jake wrestle national champion Mark Perry in the Big Ten finals, and I watched them engage in plenty of scrambles. After studying the match, I knew that he was going to be two steps behind at every turn. All of those unorthodox positions that Coach Smith had encouraged me to work on had manifested themselves into a very dynamic scrambling style that only I had mastered at that point.

Riding the bus to the arena that Saturday night, I was keeping it loose, cracking jokes, picking my hair, and having fun with the guys. I could sense Coach Smith's frustration (and maybe some anxiety), so I looked at him and said, "Hey, Coach Smith, don't worry. I'm gonna smash this guy!"

He chuckled.

In the match, Jake engaged in the scrambles, and I was always a step ahead.

My prediction was correct, and so was my preparation. All because Coach Smith encouraged it—and didn't dismiss it.

I ended up winning the match, 14-2, to become Mizzou's first national champion and fulfill the vision that Coach Smith laid out for me on my recruiting trip.

I won again in 2007, then was followed by Mark Ellis (2009) and my brother Max (2010), who started a train of many national champions at Missouri. Today, that number stands at ten.

Some may say I blazed the trail, but we all know it was Coach Smith.

–Ben Askren,
two-time NCAA Champion, 2008 Olympian

Your organization needs its own stories. It doesn't matter if you're a coach or a business leader. It doesn't matter what your sport or industry is. You need stories, like Ben Askren's story, that powerfully share the values of the culture you're trying to build. And you need to learn how to tell them well.

THE VALUE OF FAILURE

One of the values I'm always trying to instill in my wrestlers is the importance of seeing failure as part of the learning process. I need my wrestlers to be committed to continuous improvement and innovation, so they have to be willing to take their disappointments, losses, and setbacks and use them as opportunities for growth. Otherwise, they will become discouraged and lose their way.

So, I tell them stories that exemplify this approach.

For example, the famed inventor Thomas Edison reportedly failed numerous times to develop a usable lightbulb before he finally came up with a design that worked. His persistence is celebrated today. Fortunately, he had the freedom to learn from each failure, iterate, improve the design, and try again until he got it right.

Google and Apple are two corporations that have famously created workplace environments where employees are encouraged to experiment and take risks without fear of reprimand. At Google, team members are encouraged to spend 20 percent of their workweek on projects of their own choosing. During this time, they can pursue their own interests and explore new ideas. This approach has led to some groundbreaking innovations because employees are not afraid to fail. Some very successful Google products have come about as a direct result of this approach, including Gmail and AdSense.

Failure is not something to be avoided at all costs. On the contrary, failure is a necessary part of growth, innovation, and self-improvement. Moving forward requires learning from our mistakes and then focusing on the next opportunity. A baseball player with two strikes must focus on the next pitch and try to learn from the strikes, not give up because he already missed twice.

I shared earlier the importance of expecting to win. Even in the face of a failure or setback, I want my wrestlers to hold onto that expectation. Instead of being crushed by a failure, I want them to think, "I will learn from this and come back even stronger next time. And then I'm going to win."

That's exactly the attitude Ben Askren had. Even after experiencing crushing losses in his freshman and sophomore years at the NCAA finals, he never lost his confidence. Each defeat was devastating, but he kept striving, learning, growing, and expecting to win. I believe his unwavering confidence is what led him to become Missouri's first national champion wrestler.

To instill this same confidence in all of our wrestlers, I

worked with our mental performance consultant, Ben Loeb, to develop a strategy to help athletes deal with defeat. He came up with something we call the "Three Rs": reflect, regroup, and reinvest. After a match, we encourage athletes to (1) *reflect* on what they could have done better, then pause to remove emotion from the analysis; (2) *regroup* by engaging in positive self-talk/ visualization about the future; and (3) *reinvest* by taking action toward restoring their competitive spirit, while preparing for the next match.

THE THREE RS FOR DEALING WITH A LOSS

REFLECT	REGROUP	REINVEST
ACT: POSITIVE BODY LANGUAGE	FOCUS: WHAT CAN I DO TO GET TO A BETTER PLACE?	GET YOURSELF UP/ ENERGIZED
SLOW DOWN, BREATHE, TAKE THE EMOTION OUT	POSITIVE SELF-TALK	FOCUS ON THE NOW
WHAT COULD I HAVE DONE BETTER?	POSITIVE VISUALIZATION	HAVE A ROUTINE COOLDOWN

CONSTANTLY INNOVATING

We have to be constantly innovating in the face of victory *or* defeat. Many successful companies have failed because they did not continue to innovate. They grew complacent and waited too long, and the market passed them by. Think of well-known examples like Kodak, Circuit City, Blockbuster, and BlackBerry. Each of these companies was once a leader in their industries, but they failed to adapt to changing environments. Their examples serve as stark reminders of the importance of maintaining a growth mindset and continually seeking improvement.

If you fail, learn from it and improve. If you win, keep pushing to get even better for the next victory. It's true in sports and business. We must constantly innovate and improve.

When I first began coaching Ben Askren, he had an unorthodox style that many doubted would work in Division 1 wrestling. However, I coached a young man from Cornell, Glenn Walter, who wrestled a different style that was taught to him by his father who coached at Wellington C. Mepham High School in Long Island, New York. Coach John Walter was a college division runner-up in 1968 and a champion in 1969. He coached his high school team in this unorthodox style, and it made them very successful.

I would see this team at summer team camp, and they were annoying to wrestle. Having been exposed to Glenn and his father's style of wrestling in the mid-1990s helped me have an open mind about what was to come. Some years later, I recruited a young man from Wisconsin who had an unorthodox style, and I knew it could be successful from seeing it firsthand through Glenn and John.

Ben's intelligence and passion for innovation, coupled with the addition of Coach Mike Eierman, who also embraced this style, led to big success. More than just becoming the first NCAA champion from Missouri, or winning two Hodge awards, Ben revolutionized the sport of wrestling with his innovative approach.

Had I not been open to change, Ben's unique style might never have been allowed to flourish. This openness to innovation has continued to benefit our program in all facets.

I apply this approach to my own self-improvement as well.

For example, I've learned a great deal from sitting in on sports psychology classes at Mizzou taught by Dr. Rick McGuire, who was not only the Olympic sports psychologist for USA Track & Field but also our track and field coach at Mizzou. He knew that I wanted to grow as a coach, so he let me sit through his classes even though I couldn't afford to pay for them. In those early years of coaching, I was dirt-poor, but he was always supportive.

Dr. McGuire created a master's degree program called Positive Coaching. In all of his teachings, he emphasizes that thoughts affect emotions, which in turn affect our psychological response. This psychological response ultimately drives our behavior and therefore our performance. That concept really hammered home for me the importance of what we think and say because our thoughts and words ultimately determine our actions. They are directly linked. So, if we want to change a team's behavior, if we want them to start embodying the principles and values of our culture, then we have to get them thinking and speaking right.

Suppose you walk into a restaurant and the staff is rude to you and unhelpful. They might have delicious food, but you're probably going to walk out. And you almost certainly won't come back to that restaurant. Contrast that with visiting your local Chick-fil-A, where the staff are taught to greet everyone with a smile, serve good food quickly, and always respond with, "My pleasure," and "Have a blessed day." That attitude, those words, make you feel welcomed, heighten your enjoyment of the experience, and make you want to return again and again.

The way our team thinks influences the way they speak, which influences the way they act, which creates a culture that people want to be part of. Realizing this connection influenced the development of Tiger Style immensely, and I began to teach everyone—both wrestlers and staff—that each one of us had to start thinking right and speaking right if we wanted to embody the principles of Tiger Style.

This includes everything from the way we answer the phone to the way we treat *all* staff in the athletic department, including everyone from janitors to marketing personnel, from sports information staff to secretaries, from athletes in all sports to the administration. Through how we speak, how we treat people, and how we act, we reveal our standards and values. A successful organization understands this.

I often pose the question to my wrestlers: Is the way you are thinking and speaking helping your performance or hurting you? This question is central to any self-assessment. As Henry Ford said, "Whether you believe you can do a thing or not, you are right." Your mindset directly influences your actions and outcomes, so this is where self-improvement and innovation have to begin.

WALKING AND TALKING TO MYSELF

I always emphasize to my team and staff the importance of being mentally present when coming into work, the locker room, and especially the practice room. Every single person needs to be ready to learn and improve every day. I've seen student-athletes come in visibly distracted, and they'll sit in the corner looking lost. When I ask what's going on, they'll tell me about a tough college class or an unexpected test that threw them off. I remind them that they need to leave those problems outside the door.

Bringing those worries into practice affects their performance, body language, and overall well-being. It could even lead to injuries. I advise them to step out for a minute, clear their mind, and return with the right mindset. If we need to address academic issues, we do that later with the advisor, and we may arrange for extra tutoring if needed.

I need this mindset adjustment just as much as my student-athletes do, so I take walks before practice to clear my head, reflect on the day, pray, and plan for practice. I know my athletes feed off my energy, so it is important for me to come into practice with the right attitude.

I learned the importance of prayer from my father, who was my most impactful mentor. Whenever I faced challenges in life—whether in wrestling, coaching, friendships, family, or jobs—he was always there to help me reflect on what truly mattered by asking insightful questions. One question he always asked was whether or not I had prayed about it.

I remember my first state title match back in 1984. While I can't recall the specifics of the match itself, I do know I won. What stands out most in my memory, however, is the moment before the match when my dad approached me. I expected a rousing pep talk, something akin to Knute Rockne's famous football speech. Instead, he placed his hands on my shoulders and prayed for me.

He didn't mention winning. Instead, he expressed his gratitude for having a son who committed fully to his pursuits. He prayed for me to have the strength and courage to give my best and to be grateful for the opportunity in front of me. He ended by saying, "In Jesus's name, amen." Though the prayer was brief, it had a profound impact on me, reinforcing the importance of prayer in every aspect of my life.

To this day, when I go on walks before practice, I carry with me the lesson my father taught me—that prayer and seeking strength and courage from a higher power can guide me through any challenge. More than that, it can boost and empower my team.

If I come in tired or upset, it could bring the whole team down and ruin the practice. Each day matters, and my words and actions need to uplift and motivate the team. They need to create an atmosphere of excitement and positive vibes.

During these pre-practice walks, I often pray for energy, express gratitude, or seek blessings for my team's health and well-being. I also think about what I'll discuss with the team before practice. This time also serves as a break from phones, computer screens, and the busyness of life, which is so incredibly important for my mental health. In today's society, people are constantly on their phones, checking emails, messages, and social media. We have to make time to get away from all of it.

This daily escape makes me a better coach. After my walk, I'm ready to return to the practice room with positive energy, regardless of how tough my day has been.

Once I've gotten my own mind right, then I'm ready to help my team do the same. I like to start each session with a daily message, often related to Tiger Style, encompassing themes like motivation, grit, mindset, and dealing with adversity. Sometimes I read a short chapter from a book to the team, which they humorously call "Coach Smith's Story Time." One of my favorite books to read is Ryan Holiday's *Discipline Is Destiny*, particularly the chapter on Lou Gehrig, the famous New York Yankee known as the Iron Horse.

Gehrig played 2,130 consecutive games despite injuries and challenges. Hearing that always makes a big impression on the team. Hearing about Gehrig's perseverance despite the hardships of playing in the 1920s and '30s, with difficult travel and limited medical support, inspires them to push through their own minor injuries and challenges.

It all begins with having the right mindset and saying the right things. Keegan O'Toole, one of our standout wrestlers, finished third twice and won the national tournament twice, alongside U20 and U23 world titles. Once, after a particularly rough practice, he admitted feeling defeated, and he began talking negatively about his practice day. But I reminded him to adopt a positive attitude. He went back to practice with renewed focus and ended the day on a high note.

During his second year, he won his first national title despite a severe ankle sprain. He refused to let the injury hinder him and used sheer mental determination to continue wrestling at a high level. His focus and positive self-talk enabled him to push through the pain and win the championship.

In his next championship run, Keegan faced a formidable opponent he had lost to twice before. He was struggling with negative thoughts, but he used journaling to refocus and cultivate a positive mindset. This mental preparation helped him wrestle an outstanding match and secure another national title.

KEEGAN'S STORY: *PREPARED TO DIE FOR THE DREAM*

In the 2022 NCAA Championship Round Two match, I was wrestling a tough Arizona State University wrestler who had been an All-American before. I was only in my second year of college. I was more confident than ever and genuinely believed that I would win the nationals and achieve a lifelong goal of mine.

In the middle of the second period, I went for a duck-under and heard what sounded like a kernel of popcorn popping in my left ankle. When I stood up, I immediately knew something was wrong. I finished the match and won 7-0. I then ran in immense pain to the training room where our doctor examined my ankle. He said, "You sprained your ankle pretty bad."

My first response was, "I am still winning the national title, Dr. Tarbox." No matter the circumstance, I had no room or time to weep or feel sorry for myself. When I got back to the hotel, I could not hold it back anymore. I started crying and feeling sorry for myself. I began making up excuses for why it would be okay if I lost.

We had our team meeting that night, and one of my coaches told me, "This is great. You expected everything to be easy and to not go through any adversity." He made a great point; how could I expect to accomplish such a challenging task without something being thrown in my face? That night as I went to bed, I knew I had to change my mindset. It was no easy task, but I woke up that morning and genuinely believed that nothing would stop me from winning.

Coach Smith has spoken many times about belief, and I knew my belief was being tested. I had to live Tiger Style if I wanted to win this NCAA title. From then on, I did whatever it took: tape, ibuprofen, Tylenol, and a whole lot of grit. I ended up winning my next three matches with nothing but belief. I came off the mat and went into the media room, barely able to focus on the questions being asked by reporters because of the pain I was in. As the adrenaline wore off, the tape on my ankle had turned my skin red from how tight it was.

A reporter asked me how I dealt with having an injured ankle in such a difficult tournament. I responded by saying, "I was prepared to die for this dream."

–Keegan O'Toole

EXERCISE 1: *PINTEREST/VISION BOARD*

To help you (and your team) get your mind right, I recommend doing an exercise that I learned from my daughter. As I mentioned earlier, she created a Pinterest board and filled it with pictures of all the places she wanted to visit, including famous landmarks and museums all around the world. For years, the board served as both inspiration and motivation.

In recent years, she has visited many of these places, and she has pictures of herself in some of the same locations she posted on her Pinterest board years ago. Her years-long exercise in visualization and goal-setting is finally paying off.

I encourage my team to do something similar, by envisioning their goals and creating a vision board. This gives them a visual, tangible way to stay focused on their goals. Try something similar with your team. You can do this both collectively and individually.

EXERCISE 2: *SKITS*

At the start of each year, I organize a campout for our team. During the campout, we divide the team into four groups, each assigned one of the different aspects of Tiger Style living: Believe, Compete, One More, or Expect to Win. Each group is then tasked with developing a skit that illustrates what their assigned value means and what it doesn't mean. For example, Compete isn't just about stepping onto the mat; it's also about how you practice, how you attend classes, and how you take notes.

The skits are essentially stories depicting both the right and wrong ways of embodying these values, and they often lead to hilarious and insightful performances. They serve a dual purpose. First, they foster a sense of camaraderie among the team members. Second, they also help in establishing our culture. As the team watches the skits, they learn what is acceptable and what isn't in our culture.

EXERCISE 3: SENIOR TALKS

At the start of the year, I ask each senior on the team to share their experiences of living Tiger Style. These talks tend to be incredibly moving and enlightening (that's the power of good storytelling, after all). Some of these seniors, even the ones who don't usually say much, will open up and share their experiences, lessons learned, friendships made, and the support they've received along the way.

This tradition allows the seniors to pass on their wisdom to the younger members of the team. One of my favorite parts of being a coach is sitting beside the campfire, listening to our seniors share their journey. It's a powerful and inspiring experience that gives me goosebumps every time. A similar exercise could be performed in a business setting by having senior team members share their experiences with new hires.

CHAPTER 7

NEVER BE SATISFIED

W HEN I USED to teach history, I always liked to tell my students about Abraham Lincoln and the many adversities he faced before becoming president. Lincoln experienced a long string of personal and professional setbacks, including numerous political defeats. He failed in business in 1833, lost his sweetheart in 1835, had a nervous breakdown in 1836, and was defeated twice when running for the Senate (1854 and 1858), among other challenges.[2]

Despite this, he kept pushing forward, reaching further, and eventually, he became president in 1860. He is now regarded as one of our greatest presidents due to his steady and decisive leadership during the Civil War. Lincoln is quoted as saying, "My great concern is not whether you have failed, but whether you are content with your failure."

I WILL NOT BE DENIED

I often share this story about Lincoln with my wrestlers because it's such a clear and compelling example of how difficult times can be not merely overcome but transformed into success, as long as we never settle. In fact, I tell my team and fellow coaches that failure is a natural part of the path to success. Losing is easy, which is why we all experience it sooner or later, but winning is hard. Winning requires perseverance and never being satisfied.

2   "Lincoln's 'Failures'?" Abraham Lincoln Online (website), accessed August 14, 2024, https://www.abrahamlincolnonline.org/lincoln/education/failures.htm

J'den Cox won the NCAA championship as a nineteen-year-old freshman. His dominance on the mat led many to believe that he might never lose again in college. However, as he entered his sophomore year, my coaching staff and I noticed subtle changes in his focus and discipline, both on and off the mat. These small lapses accumulated, and he lost twice at the NCAA championships that year, which prevented him from achieving four national titles.

J'den's attitude changed dramatically again in his junior year, this time for the better. He recommitted himself to leadership and excellence, and as a result, he ultimately won the NCAA championship at Madison Square Garden. Following this victory, I informed him that he needed to compete in the Olympic trials, which were scheduled for two weeks later. He was initially reluctant due to sheer mental and physical exhaustion, but the coaching staff eventually persuaded him to seize the opportunity. Entering the trials as the ninth seed, he defeated four opponents to make the 2016 Olympic team, later winning a bronze medal in Brazil.

This transformation continued into his senior year, despite the grueling schedule of competing in the Olympics and fulfilling numerous speaking engagements. His popularity and the demands on his time were immense, and all the more so because J'den has a hearing impairment, which made him a role model for hearing-impaired students. To keep him from getting burned out, I insisted he take two weeks off in January, a decision he initially resisted but later benefited from.

As the season progressed, J'den's dedication remained unwavering. One cold morning in February, I spotted a lone figure running across campus and later discovered it was J'den running to practice. He ran three miles and showed up drenched in sweat. When I asked why he would exert himself so much before a demanding workout, he simply replied, "I never want to be satisfied, Coach. I will not be denied my national title."

His determination paid off, and he ended his college career by winning his third NCAA title his senior year. J'den Cox truly embodied the resilience and relentless pursuit of excellence that I strive to instill in all of my athletes.

J'DEN'S STORY: **PUSHING PAST MY LIMITS**

Truth be told, I hate to run. It has never been something I was quite good at, let alone felt good doing. I have never understood people who say they feel good running or do it recreationally. However, in 2016, my perspective changed a little bit. Running became a time for me to envision myself pushing past my limits on the mat.

You see, I do not visualize my opponents; I only see myself. I run and push myself, repeating phrases like "keep moving," "hands move, feet move," "do not stop, do not slow down." All kinds of things. Running became my method of recreating the feeling of matches even before they occurred. When I say "feeling," I mean exactly that. I would feel the pain from running in my knees, arms, lungs, all over my body, and I would visualize myself in a match with this pain and say, "Okay, now wrestle." When the weather is bad, it acts as a physical representation of an opponent.

The day I found out I love running in rough weather was a winter day when Missouri experienced blizzard-like conditions. The snow was relentless, but I still had to go to practice. At the time, the house I stayed in was about 3.5 miles away. I had to be more focused with each step in the snow. My purpose was even clearer as the wind tried to push me off course, and my body had to push through the cold that felt like it was trying to stop me. Bear in mind, this was still all just to get to practice.

I remember running in and finally getting to the Hearnes Center locker room. I did not tell anyone I ran it; I was not looking for a pat on the back or anything. Then, as I stood at my locker covered in wet snow, I heard, "J'den, what were you doing?" I turned around, and I saw Coach Smith.

I responded, "I just ran in from my house," to which he said, "That was you?" Obviously, he had seen me passing through the snow in my all-black outfit. I nodded my head, and then his last question was, "Why would you do that?"

I just told the truth: "Nobody is going to beat me this year. Nobody is going to take that national title from me again. Nobody is going to outwork me."

And so, I got dressed for practice.

–J'den Cox,
three-time NCAA Champion, 2016 Olympic Bronze
Medalist

GET BACK OUT THERE

I learned the value of never being satisfied from my father. During my first year of wrestling varsity as a sophomore at Oviedo High School, I was eager for a big win. I had never beaten a state placer before, and I found myself facing an opponent who had finished fourth in the state the previous year and was currently ranked second. I knew this was going to be a real test of my progress, so I gave it everything I had.

Miraculously, I managed to win the match. I was exhilarated and felt like I was on top of the world as I headed home.

My sisters had a bunch of their friends over, and I reveled in my victory, strutting around the house with my chest puffed out, basking in all the compliments.

But then I noticed my dad standing on the other side of the living room, watching me with a thoughtful expression. I could tell he wanted to say something. Finally, he walked over to me, gave me a stern look, and said, "Are you satisfied with that?"

Confused, I replied, "You mean the win today?"

"Yes," he said, "are you satisfied with that?"

It seemed like a trick question, so I took a deep breath and answered carefully, "No, I'm not satisfied."

My father nodded and said, "You damn well better not be, because that guy's out there right now working out while you're goofing off with your sisters and bragging. He's going to come back more prepared for you, so you'd better get back out there and keep improving."

My dad's words were a life lesson on never being satisfied, no matter the success. That moment stuck with me deeply. It taught me that complacency is the enemy of progress. Whether in wrestling, teaching, coaching, or fatherhood, I have learned that you must keep striving for improvement, always preparing for the next challenge. This lesson has stayed with me throughout my life, and I continue to pass it on to my teams.

We have to constantly reach for the next achievement, and never become complacent about meeting the high standards we've set for ourselves. It all comes down to the habits we develop. The way we conduct ourselves, whether we win, lose, or face a tough day in practice, is a product of the habits we've developed over time.

That's another reason why I am constantly trying to instill these values into the small, routine actions of my staff and team.

From the way athletes dress for practice to the way staff handle phone calls or write notes to recruits, I want our commitment to constant improvement to be evident. I want us to never be afraid of asking questions and seeking growth. I want my wrestlers to attend every class and strive to learn as much as possible, working hard to become the best teammates they can be and adopting an attitude that everything is our responsibility.

The moment we think we can slack off or let something slip without consequence, we lower our standards. Winning is contagious, but so is losing. Living right must be a daily commitment. Again, that's why I constantly emphasize the concept of One More. It's a way of making sure that we are all—staff and team—constantly seeking improvement, never letting complacency set in. The phrase "One More" gives us a name for this behavior so that we can talk about it constantly.

For example, you might hear someone at practice say, "Hey, you want to do one more?" Or a student talking about their grades might say, "I currently have a B, but I'm trying to do one more to raise it to an A."

Never be satisfied. Always strive to do a little more, achieve a little more, reach a little further. Get back out there and keep pushing. That's the only way to truly achieve greatness. You can't be satisfied with merely doing what's expected of you. Today's wins *and* losses both must propel you toward the next great opportunity.

That's why, after a good phone call with a recruit, I don't want my staff to be content. I want them to follow up with a personal note. Even small actions like these are part and parcel of an attitude of always doing a little more.

To create a successful culture that wins, you have to set high standards and do everything you can to encourage people to constantly seek a competitive edge. I remember on one occasion, I had my wrestlers running laps in the practice room, and Alan Waters intentionally stuck to the outermost edge of the room. He wanted to give himself a little bit of additional challenge, but even so, he was still outpacing everyone. Alan's consistent One More attitude helped him become a two-time All-American at Mizzou and influenced his teammates to follow him and push themselves.

EXERCISE: **ONE MORE**

To create a culture of excellence for your team, I recommend the following exercise. Break your team into small groups, and have each group discuss three things that could hinder your team's ability to succeed. Afterward, have them share their thoughts and identify any related issues that the team needs to address right away.

During these same meetings, you can talk about what One More means for your organization and publicly recognize individuals and groups when they go the extra mile. We've even organized One More competitions, where we split the team into groups and assign points for actions like helping others or doing extra work. The group competition goes on over a number of days, and then we acknowledge and reward the winners at the end. It boosts enthusiasm, fosters teamwork, and develops leadership.

These One More group exercises help embed this mentality into the daily routines of our team members and staff so that it influences our habits. We should all be constantly pushing to reach new heights in everything we do, and this must be evident in the way we approach every day.

CHAPTER 8

EXPECT TO WIN

ANOTHER ONE OF the core values in Tiger Style culture is Expect to Win, which refers to confidence that is strengthened by strong relationships and a conviction that success is always achievable. My team lives this value by always giving their best effort, no matter the odds.

Of course, expecting to win requires preparation. The more you prepare, the more confident you become. That's why we require our wrestlers to attend every single class. The connection between attending class and wrestling performance might not be clear, but here's the thing: When our wrestlers attend class, it alleviates stress during exam periods. And those exam periods often coincide with major competitions like the NCAAs.

I constantly remind the team that consistent attendance during the fall and spring semesters will set them up for success. If they stay on top of their studies, they will manage their time better, and that will prevent them from falling behind. As a result, they will be less stressed, less discouraged, and able to give their best in every area of life.

Preparation extends beyond academics, of course. It involves consistently doing all the small things right, such as extra practice sessions. These One Mores turn weaknesses into strengths and build confidence in techniques that can be executed flawlessly in matches. Thorough preparation ensures that athletes are not merely reacting to situations but are anticipating them and know instinctively how to respond.

Preparation is just as important for coaches. My coaching staff and I try to meticulously plan for every scenario. We prepare for warm-ups and strategize for second and third overtimes in wrestling matches. We discuss contingencies for injuries and determine who will fill in for an injured teammate. This level of preparation prevents last-minute panic and ensures that everyone knows their role.

Meticulous planning also applies to travel and competition logistics. I work closely with my director of operations to ensure our athletes are ready for anything when it comes to travel. We've learned the hard way that things like bad weather and flight delays can lead to late arrivals that disrupt our preparation. We make sure our athletes are equipped with practice gear in their carry-ons in case of lost luggage, and we bring nutritious food for potential delays. Arriving late and scrambling to find a practice facility is not ideal, so we prioritize practicing before departure. These measures ensure that the team is always ready, no matter the circumstances.

Preparation also means having a strategy for handling setbacks. I learned an important lesson from a bitter confrontation with Tyron Woodley, future UFC champion. After a disappointing match, I was too swift with my criticism, and he didn't take it well. However, that incident taught me the importance of timing and approach when providing feedback. Now, I focus on starting with positive reinforcement before addressing areas for needed improvement.

Mentorship plays an important role in building confidence as well. By seeking advice from experienced individuals outside of our immediate circle, we gain new perspectives. I frequently consult other coaches at Mizzou, our team doctor, and my brother, a successful businessman. Their insights help me stay focused on the processes that lead to success, rather than being solely results-oriented.

THE RIGHT ATTITUDE

When I say, "Expect to Win," I'm not talking about being willfully confident no matter the odds. I'm talking about a confidence that comes from thorough preparation, strategic planning, and continuous learning. By focusing on the processes that lead to success, we build a strong foundation for achieving our goals, both in sports and in life. That's what Expect to Win means.

When everything is well prepared and organized, you feel naturally confident because you know all contingencies have been covered. Being organized instills a belief that you are prepared for any situation, which enables you to be truly confident of victory. Expect to Win is based on reasonable certainty and careful preparation.

Of course, losses do happen, and when they do, we need to have a plan for handling them. In individual sports like wrestling, an athlete can take a loss especially hard. I've seen plenty of wrestlers storm off in frustration. As I said, I always try to focus on positive reinforcement before addressing areas for improvement, but even then, it's a focus on processes, not just results.

I believe a similar attitude is important in business. The emphasis should be on creating a quality product rather than merely chasing profits. Cheating the system for short-term gains undermines long-term success. But if you focus on creating a quality product and delivering value to customers, then you can be reasonably confident of becoming profitable.

I still vividly remember the first press conference I ever gave as a wrestling coach at Mizzou. As I started talking about my plans and aspirations for the team, it soon became clear that the audience found my big dreams hard to believe. There were some, especially the journalism students from our esteemed journalism school, who made no effort to hide their skepticism. They seemed to think, "Who is this young coach making grand claims about winning Big 12s and achieving success when the wrestling team historically has never performed well at any time?"

Some of them even snickered at me, as if I were naïve or crazy. But I had enough confidence in the process I would instill, and I fully expected to start winning. More importantly, I knew our victories weren't going to come out of thin air; they would be the product of a well-organized plan for creating a successful culture. Little did the skeptics that day know we were at the very beginning of a journey that was going to lead to some truly impressive accomplishments.

THE POWER OF DETERMINATION

John Andrews's story is a testament to success born not of blind ambition but the power of determination and personal development. John was an English major and artist who was deeply involved in his art classes, but he also wrestled on our team. Although he wasn't a starter, he lettered twice and earned the title of First Team Academic All-Big 12.

However, after college, John turned his aspirations toward getting into medical school, and his confidence about his future plans stemmed largely from the lessons he learned through wrestling. We helped him develop a competitive spirit and a willingness to go above and beyond, qualities that were instrumental in his pursuit of his dream career.

After graduating from college, John traveled around Europe for a while. When he returned home, he paid me a visit at my office and announced his plan to attend medical school. Initially, I was skeptical. During the years I'd known him, John had been deeply involved in art and English, not science. However, instead of discouraging him, I asked if he had taken any science classes. He admitted he had, though he hadn't excelled in them. Even so, he remained determined, and more importantly, he had made careful preparations for achieving his goal.

John outlined his plan, which involved taking additional science classes and internships. Despite the challenges and the significant financial burden of living in Manhattan, he enrolled in a program at Columbia University to complete the necessary science coursework. After two years, he began applying to medical schools and asked for my recommendation for some prestigious institutions, including Yale. To be completely honest, I doubted his chances of getting in, but John's determination prevailed.

Remarkably, he was accepted into Yale Medical School, where he excelled, graduating near the top of his class and winning numerous awards. He was then accepted into a prestigious neurosurgery residency at the University of California, San Francisco, one of the top hospitals for neurosurgery in the country. Now in his seventh year, John continues to excel.

John attributes much of his success to the discipline and commitment he learned from wrestling. The Tiger Style philosophy and values and our training environment cultivated his belief in himself and his ability to achieve great things through hard work, good habits, and careful preparation. In a more general sense, his story is a powerful example of how the lessons learned in sports can translate into success in all areas of life when we embrace an Expect to Win mindset.

Here is John's story in his own words:

JOHN'S STORY: *FROM WRESTLING TO NEUROSURGERY*

After I finished my five years as a Missouri Tiger, there was a period of time when I felt like a failure. As a freshman, I was a walk-on to the wrestling team, having not been highly recruited. While I had not won a state championship in high school, I thought I still had something to prove. College wrestling was my next chance to prove that I was as good as I thought I was.

In the Tigers wrestling room, I was surrounded by people who either had already achieved greatness or were in the process of it. It felt like everyone was better than me. I had some successes in my college wrestling career, but I had many, many failures. Despite the failures, I never let myself quit. That was the line I would not cross. At the end of my college career, by many of the standards that were held up by the team, I had failed. I was not a national champion nor an All-American. It hurt.

After college, I decided to shift the focus of my life away from wrestling. I floundered a bit during that first year. I traveled, pursued art for a time, and did some soul-searching. However, I felt lost without a goal to strive for or a title to work toward. I wanted a career I could take pride in to replace what wrestling had been in my life. My losses in wrestling still haunted me. Whenever I felt too low, however, I thought about standing with the handful of teammates who remained from our large recruiting class after five long years of Division 1 wrestling. I had stuck it out when much more decorated wrestlers had not.

I realized that even without the titles I craved, this perseverance was an achievement and a skill in itself. I knew how to work hard for years at a time, with little reward along the way, toward a goal that seemed out of reach. I had proved I could do hard things in wrestling, so I decided to put that skill set into practice.

I decided to go to medical school, partly because of the reputation medicine had for demanding long years of hard work. Despite not taking the required premed courses in college, and knowing it was going to be a years-long transition, I was not as intimidated as I might have been without my background in college wrestling. I knew what it felt like to put in years of work toward something—this was my strength, and it was the foundation I could use to build myself up from an English major and a wrestler into a competitive medical school applicant.

I found post-baccalaureate programs that were designed to let me take the college coursework required to apply to medical school. When I needed a letter of recommendation, I reached out to my coach because I had faith that after the years of work I put in for him, he would support me however he could. When I got into Columbia University's post-baccalaureate program, I treated school the way I wished I had treated college wrestling: I made it my job.

I modeled my studying habits after the wrestling training regimens of my successful teammates in college. I found ways to study all the time. I treated every test like a wrestling tournament—I put in the work during the days, weeks, and months leading up to tests so that the test itself was nothing new. I knew from wrestling that matches were won in the months and years of training that preceded them. I lived and breathed studying. I found mentors who were successful in academic medicine and got their advice. I also treated medical school applications the way I wish I had treated wrestling.

I lived this transformation for three years—two years of coursework followed by a full year of medical school applications. By the end, I had transformed myself into a stellar medical school applicant.

It was a plan that worked. When I was accepted to Yale for medical school, I realized I had done something special. I had translated skills from the wrestling room into a completely different field. Once I saw the results of this philosophy, I didn't want to stop. I decided I wanted to go into neurosurgery. It was a field that treated some of the most complex diseases known to humanity. It had a reputation for demanding the most work of any medical specialty. After what I had done in wrestling, work was not something I would let get in my way. I didn't feel like a freshman walk-on anymore! I had turned myself into a blue-chip recruit.

I spent my time in medical school retooling myself into a neuroscientist and a prospective neurosurgeon. The work ethic I'd learned in wrestling endeared me to my mentors. I was willing to take on the hardest, most complex projects. I was willing to put in the hours—and I didn't even have to cut weight. With the support of my mentors and again from my college wrestling coach, I applied to the most competitive neurosurgical residency programs in the country. Every single neurosurgery residency interviewer I talked to brought up my wrestling background and loved it. Something about this philosophy translated perfectly into neurosurgery. I was one of three applicants accepted to what is widely considered the top neurosurgery residency in the country, the University of California, San Francisco.

What started as a technique to get into med school has turned into my lifestyle. Now, in my seventh and final year of neurosurgery residency training, people still know me as the wrestler. I joke with colleagues that my real major in college was wrestling because that was my most valuable curriculum. The lessons I learned as a Missouri Tiger are the lessons I used to launch my career, and I feel like I finally earned the title I was looking for all along.

–John P. Andrews, MD

CONSISTENT COMMITMENT TO EXCELLENCE

Dom Bradley was a successful wrestler with a lifelong expectation to win. He recently retired from wrestling at the age of thirty-five, which is an unusually late retirement for such a physically demanding sport.

He approached life consistently, from high school through his time at Mizzou as a two-time All-American. He was always confident and driven, and as a result, he only got better over time. I always said he was like a fine wine: The older he got, the better he wrestled. He later returned to coach at Mizzou, even while he was still training for the Olympics.

I remember telling him a few years ago, "Dom, you're an exceptional coach, but the more you coach, the better you wrestle." Dom agreed and explained that teaching and breaking down techniques for others had made him better at using those techniques himself. Coaching deepened his understanding of the sport and improved his performance both as a competitor and a coach.

Dom retired recently after placing fourth at the 2024 Olympic trials, which earned him a spot on the national team. He could have continued. He was certainly good enough, but he realized he needed to focus on coaching and his family. Still, his story is a testament to someone who achieved great things by living his life with a consistent commitment to excellence and a constant expectation to win.

Kenny Burleson's journey was equally inspiring. Kenny was part of my first recruiting class at Mizzou, a skinny kid from Neosho, Missouri. Initially recruited as a 125-pounder, Kenny grew into a 157-pounder by his senior year. Though he never won a wrestle-off to start the season, Kenny's performance in tournaments earned him a starting spot. Despite a few initial losses, he eventually competed with All-Americans and steadily improved. Academically, he excelled with an almost perfect GPA, and later in life, he made significant strides in business.

Kenny became a four-time Academic All-American. In his senior year, he defeated a high-quality wrestler from Oklahoma State, won the Big 12 Championship, and became an All-American. As part of the first class that bought into Tiger Style, Kenny was a perfect example of dedication, determination, and preparation. He captained the team with Jeremy Spates, and through it all, he constantly embodied the values of Tiger Style through his training, academics, and community service.

During his senior year, he placed fifth. It was a frustrating end to his time on our team, and Kenny broke down, sobbing and apologizing for not winning the NCAA championship. Shocked and upset for him, I held him like a parent holds a hurt child. I reassured him that he had done more for our program than he realized. Kenny's performance and commitment had made me incredibly proud. We hugged and cried for ten minutes, knowing it was our last moment together as coach and athlete. It was a special moment with someone who had fully embraced Tiger Style, and it was meaningful for me because he had been part of my first recruiting class.

More than anything else, it's the changes I've seen in my wrestlers, the personal growth and development that endure long after they've graduated and left the program, that make Tiger Style so powerful. Guys like Kenny Burleson, Dom Bradley, J'Den Cox, John Andrews, Mark Ellis, Todd Schavrien, Keegan O'Toole, and Ben Askren testify to the power of our culture of *believing*, *competing*, always doing *one more*, and *expecting to win*.

EXERCISE 1: **CATCHPHRASE**

One simple exercise I like to do to instill an expectation to win in my team is to take some important quote, acronym, or statement from a book like *ACE Your Way* by Ben Loeb, have it printed, and then share it with the team. We discuss what it means and how it relates to our program. You can do something similar in almost any setting using a quote that is meaningful to your team or business culture. This encourages positive thinking and reflection.

EXERCISE 2: **JOURNALING**

Journaling is a powerful exercise that I practice myself and that I have encouraged my wrestlers to adopt. Have each team member write in their journal their routine for success in competition, sales, or any other area. Then have them reflect on *why* they expect to succeed tomorrow, including what they have done to prepare for success.

If they are not prepared or confident about success, they can evaluate what changes need to be made. They might even list three specific things that will give them a better chance of success. Finally, have them write ways they can help other team members elevate their performance.

This kind of journaling creates regular self-reflection, which is important for maintaining high standards and constantly seeking improvement.

CONCLUSION

A s I NEAR the conclusion of my coaching career, I find myself reminiscing about my journey and all the experiences that have shaped my time in this role. I can tell you what I will miss *least* about this job: the time away from my family. The demands of college athletics have only intensified over the years, especially with the rise of the transfer portal, which has introduced a new season dedicated solely to recruiting. The expansion of the portal and the advent of name, image, and likeness (NIL) opportunities mean that coaches are now constantly seeking support from businesses and individuals to bolster their programs.

This transformation in college sports, which has brought about high transfer rates and diminishing loyalty to schools and programs, has made it increasingly difficult to cultivate long-term relationships and a robust culture. While the challenge is not insurmountable, it has added a lot more time, pressure, and complexity to the task of nurturing an environment where culture can thrive. I won't miss that, but I hope the younger generation of coaches "find a way" to create their Tiger Style–like culture in this changing environment.

On the other hand, I *will* miss the connections forged with my staff and student-athletes. I cherish the memories I have of traveling with the team, even during the most arduous times. Despite many challenges, we always find ways to inject fun into the experience. I will long for those times when the team gathers for meals during Thanksgiving or Christmas, which makes training sessions over the holidays a tad more enjoyable.

I'll also miss our traditional team events, like the campout during the first week of school, where we pitch tents, share meals, and hold our inaugural team meeting around a crackling fire. The seniors impart wisdom about what Tiger Style means to them and encourage newcomers to savor every moment because time passes swiftly. The following day's rafting trips, where upperclassmen playfully tease freshmen by snatching their oars, are always a highlight, especially when my sons can join us.

While I may not miss the complaints and disputes over rules, I will fondly recall the spirited competition that characterizes our daily kickball games before practice. I will miss the senior talks at our year-end banquet, where our athletes express their love for the program and gratitude for those who supported them. Witnessing their growth into eloquent public speakers over their tenure here has always filled me with admiration.

I will also miss the process of nurturing young men, instilling in them the principles of Tiger Style, and the gratification I feel after a productive practice session, when I know we have made strides that day. The practice room has served as more than just a venue for team-building. It has been a crucible where young men transform into leaders and empathetic teammates. While I impart a lot of knowledge, my staff and team also teach *me* many invaluable lessons.

I will sorely miss the battles and competitions. The pre-match intensity in the locker room, the unwavering confidence of our young men, the electrifying atmosphere of duals at the Hearnes Center with fervent crowds—these moments are forever etched in my memory. I know that in the years ahead, I will yearn for the camaraderie following a big victory and the emotional embrace after hard-fought losses or when an athlete ascends to All-American, national champion, or Olympian status. These poignant moments will endure within me.

Guiding this program for nearly three decades has been an honor. I am thankful for the privilege of waking up each day to pursue something I feel truly passionate about. Some of my most cherished moments include receiving texts and photos from parents expressing gratitude for fulfilling my promise to them when their son graduated, as well as receiving warm embraces from parents who tell me they can't imagine their sons anywhere else.

There are so many moments that I will always cherish as a coach, especially now that my father has passed. We had a wrestler on our team struggling with the possibility of losing his father, who had been battling ALS. Despite being unable to speak, this father had not missed a single one of his son's matches. On one occasion, he drove ten hours to witness his son compete at Oklahoma State.

It was a hard-fought dual, and this young man's win sealed the victory for us. In the locker room, emotions were running high because winning in Stillwater had not been accomplished by too many teams. As I stepped outside to collect my thoughts, I witnessed the father embracing his son—tears and hugs were exchanged, not merely for the win, but for the opportunity to share in that moment together. That's the kind of thing that will stay with me for the rest of my life.

My devotion to this program will never waver, and I will continue to support future Tigers. I will continue to attend weddings, reconnect at team gatherings, and always delight in hearing from former athletes. We are always striving to win, but I hope from reading this book, you have learned that being a coach is more about the role I get to play in shaping their character and work ethic. When they affirm that they are still embodying Tiger Style, I am reminded of why I chose to coach.

In this book, I have shared how Tiger Style evolved into the cultural ethos of the wrestling program at Mizzou. In doing so, I hope that I have inspired you to cultivate your own Tiger Style culture within your team or business. Culture triumphs when individuals embrace a shared vision, strive for it each day, give a little extra, and always anticipate victory.

BELIEVE, COMPETE, ONE MORE, EXPECT TO WIN

Create your culture, and live it out daily. That's what I've tried to do throughout my coaching career. In fact, I want my tombstone to say, "He lived Tiger Style. Every day."

RECOMMENDED READING

Here are some of the books I have read, and I did my own categorizing so you can read something for the right topic. Enjoy.

MENTAL

The Champion's Mind	Afremow, Jim
Funky: My Defiant Path through the Wild World of Combat Sports	Askren, Ben
Mindset: The New Psychology of Success	Dweck, Carol S.
Range	Epstein, David
The Sports Gene	Epstein, David
The Tipping Point	Gladwell, Malcom
Stay Sane in an Insane World	Harden, Greg, and Steve Hamilton
The Compound Effect	Hardy, Darren
Stillness Is the Key	Holiday, Ryan
Endure	Hutchinson, Alex

Think Like a Freak	Levitt, Steven D., and Stephen J. Dubner
Zen Golf	Parent, Joseph
212 The Extra Degree	Parker, Sam, and Mac Anderson
Winning the Mental Game	Selking, Amber
Start with Why	Sinek, Simon
The Infinite Game	Sinek, Simon
Develop the Predator Mindset: Win in Sports and Life	Zannetti, Gene

CULTURE

Across the River	Babb, Kent
How the Mighty Fall	Collins, Jim C.
Flip the Script	Cooper, Coyte
Make Your Mark	Cooper, Coyte
The Culture Code	Coyle, Daniel
Uncommon	Dungy, Tony
The Soul of a Team	Dungy, Tony

The Sale	Gordon, Jon, and Alex Demczak
The Coffee Bean	Gordon, Jon, and Damon West
You Win in the Locker Room First	Gordon, Jon, and Mike Smith
Soup	Gordon, Jon
The Energy Bus	Gordon, Jon
The Garden	Gordon, Jon
The Seed	Gordon, Jon
Made to Stick	Heath, Chip, and Dan Heath
Switch: How to Change Things When Change is Hard	Heath, Chip, and Dan Heath
The Power of Moments	Heath, Chip, and Dan Heath
Right Thing, Right Now	Holiday, Ryan
The Obstacle Is the Way	Holiday, Ryan
The Dream Manager	Kelly, Matthew
The Generosity Habit	Kelly, Matthew
Legacy	Kerr, James

What Drives Winning Environments	Ledbetter, Brett
What Drives Winning Teams	Ledbetter, Brett
The Five Dysfunctions of a Team	Lencioni, Patrick
The Real Madrid Way	Mandis, Steven G.
The Other Wes Moore	Moore, Wes
The Last Lecture	Pausch, Randy
The Warrior Ethos	Pressfield, Steven

COACHING

Remembering Herbie	Bernstein, Ross
Coach: 25 Writers Reflect on People Who Made a Difference	Blauner, Andrew
Win Forever	Carroll, Pete
A Most Beautiful Thing	Cooper, Arshay
Getting to Us	Davis, Seth
The Way of the SEAL	Divine, Mark
Quiet Strength	Dungy, Tony
The Mentor Leader	Dungy, Tony

InSideOut Coaching	Ehrmann, Joe
A Wrestling Life	Gable, Dan
Talk Like TED	Gallo, Carmine
David and Goliath	Gladwell, Malcolm
The Power of a Positive Team	Gordon, Jon
The Power of Positive Leadership	Gordon, Jon
Not All Roads Lead to Gold	Gruenwald, Jim
Be Quick but Don't Hurry	Hill, Andrew
Discipline Is Destiny	Holiday, Ryan
Winning Every Day	Holtz, Lou
The Twin Thieves: How Great Leaders Build Great Teams	Jones, Steve, and Lucas Jadin
Leading with the Heart	Krzyzewski, Mike
The Gold Standard: Building a World-Class Team	Krzyzewski, Mike
ACE Your Way	Loeb, Ben
Next-Level Coaching	Loeb, Ben
The Lombardi Rules	Lombardi Jr., Vince

Fathers & Sons & Sports	Lupica, Mike
Story Selling: Sage Advice and Common Sense about Sales and Success	Maziar, Harry
4th and Goal	McCartney, Bill
Above the Line	Meyer, Urban
Do It Anyway	Miller, Jim
Belichick	O'Connor, Ian
Every Moment Matters	O'Sullivan, John
Game Changing Moves	Parks, Chad
The 100-Yard Journey: A Life in Coaching and Battling for the Win	Pinkel, Gary
The Thursday Speeches	Tormey, Peter G.
The Score Takes Care of Itself	Walsh, Bill

LEADERSHIP

Being George Washington	Beck, Glenn
The Leadership Lessons of Jesus	Briner, Bob, and Ray Pritchard

How to Win Friends and Influence People	Carnegie, Dale
Greatness	Cook, David L.
The Edge	Ferguson, Howard E.
Lead . . . for God's Sake!	Gongwer, Todd
The Compassionate Samurai	Klemmer, Brian
In Extremis Leadership	Kolditz, Thomas, A.
Turn the Ship Around!	Marquet, L. David
Be All You Can Be	Maxwell, John C.
Intentional Living	Maxwell, John C.
Leadershift	Maxwell, John C.
Leadership Gold	Maxwell, John C.
Running with the Giants	Maxwell, John C.
The 21 Indispensable Qualities of a Leader	Maxwell, John C.
The 21 Irrefutable Laws of Leadership	Maxwell, John C.
The 5 Levels of Leadership	Maxwell, John C.

Team of Teams	McChrystal, Stanley
QBQ! The Question Behind the Question	Miller, John G.
The Leadership Game	Mullins, Tom
The Leader Who Had No Title	Sharma, Robin
The Monk Who Sold His Ferrari	Sharma, Robin
Leaders Eat Last	Sinek, Simon
Together Is Better	Sinek, Simon
The Art of War	Tzu, Sun
Beyond Winning: The Timeless Wisdom of Great Philosopher Coaches	Walton, Gary M.
Through the Banks of the Red Cedar	Washington, Maya

BOOKS MY ATHLETES HAVE ENJOYED

The Boys in the Boat	Brown, Daniel James
Legends of the Mat	Chapman, Mike
The Power of One	Courtenay, Bryce
Advice from Champions	DeStefanis, Ken

Life to the Fullest	Donnelly, Darrin
Old School Grit	Donnelly, Darrin
The Mental Game	Donnelly, Darrin
The Turnaround	Donnelly, Darrin
One Word That Will Change Your Life	Gordon, Jon
The Hard Hat	Gordon, Jon
The No Complaining Rule	Gordon, Jon
Breathe: A Life in Flow	Gracie, Rickson
Bleachers	Grisham, John
The History of Collegiate Wrestling	Hammond, Jairus K.
Shoe Dog	Knight, Phil
Season of Life	Marx, Jeffrey
24: Life Stories and Lessons from the Say Hey Kid	Mays, Willie, and John Shea
Make Your Bed	McRaven, William H.
Chop Wood Carry Water	Medcalf, Joshua

Pound the Stone	Medcalf, Joshua
The Red Bandana	Rinaldi, Tom
The Fisherman: Leadership Traits to Win the Game of Life	Steckel, Dave
This Is the Day	Tebow, Tim

ACKNOWLEDGMENTS

ACKNOWLEDGING ALL THE people who made this book possible is a challenge since so many people have influenced me and supported me. My parents are first because they always let me chase my dreams. Heck, they moved the entire family from Binghamton, New York, to Florida because of my health. That family sacrifice is still a motivating, driving force in my life. My brother and two sisters were a part of that sacrifice, and I am indebted to them.

I also have to mention all of those coaches who inspired me over the years, from my cousin Kevin Smith, who introduced me to wrestling, to Randy Miller, my senior-year high school coach, who opened my eyes to the sport of wrestling.

To mentors/friends like Coach Rob Koll and Jack Spates and the many assistant coaches and staff I have worked with who believed in and helped bring Tiger Style to life: It was an honor to work with all of you. We went through many long days and highs and lows of the seasons, but I will always cherish the relationships that were formed.

Dr. Bus Tarbox, my team doctor and long-time friend; my brother, Terry Smith; my director of operations, Keenan Hagerty; and my son Quinn, who all took the time to assist me with this book by supporting me, reading, and reminding me that Tiger Style's message is important. Also, my former Syracuse wrestler and author Rob Buyea for his invaluable support, advice, and time.

To my wife, who never knew what it meant to be a coach's wife before marrying me. You have not only embraced it, you continue to do so much to support me, to support the program, and of course, to be the glue of our family. I hear people call Denise "Mrs. Tiger Style," and she has earned that title for sure. I could not have succeeded in coaching without her love, friendship, and support. My children, Quinn, Kylie, and Braden, have always inspired me in different ways and kept me centered. Coming home from practice or long road trips and spending time with them is still the highlight of my day.

Tiger Style is a culture, but it evolved from a group of people believing in the vision that we set in motion back in the early 2000s. In 2023, when I met Alex Demczak at a Mizzou football game, he happened to be an author and a part of Streamline Books, and I told him my vision for a book. Whether it was fate we met that day or luck, it happened, and all the people at Streamline Books helped make this dream a reality.

Lastly, to all the young men whom I have had the privilege to coach, for their unwavering sacrifice and belief each day in the practice room, weight room, classroom, and competition, and still today in whatever adventure they have moved on to. Without them, there would be no reason to create Tiger Style. Without them, a group of people would not have turned a "Belief" into everyday work and "Competed" for it. Without them driving themselves to do "One More," we wouldn't have a culture of confident young men who "Expect to Win." Without them, there is no Tiger Style.

It is very difficult to properly acknowledge everyone, but to all who took part in this, thanks for your support in bringing Tiger Style to life.

ABOUT THE AUTHOR

SINCE HIS APPOINTMENT as the University of Missouri's head wrestling coach on May 5, 1998, Brian Smith has demanded excellence from himself, his coaches, and his wrestlers. Under his leadership, the Tigers have transformed in a remarkable way. His unique "Tiger Style" culture turned a struggling team into a national powerhouse, consistently ranked among the top ten in the nation.

Smith inherited a program that hadn't seen a winning record since the 1991-92 season and led the Tigers to twenty-three consecutive seasons with a dual record of .500 or better starting in 2001-02. He has coached thirty-one All-Americans to sixty-eight top-eight finishes and six wrestlers to nine national championships.

In each of his twenty-six seasons at Missouri, at least one Tiger wrestler has competed at the NCAA Championships, with the team finishing among the top twenty programs in nineteen of the last twenty seasons. Missouri saw a program-high five All-Americans at the national tournaments in 2009, 2015, 2017, and 2023.

Since 1998, fifty-three wrestlers under Smith have been recognized for their academic achievements by the National Wrestling Coaches Association (NWCA), Big 12, and College Sports Communicators (formerly CoSIDA). The program's success has generated excitement and interest in wrestling, both in Columbia and nationally. Smith and his team have attracted record crowds to the Hearnes Center, consistently ranking among the top twenty-five programs in attendance, averaging over 2,000 spectators per home dual. On February 4, 2024, against third-ranked Oklahoma State, the Tigers drew 6,207 fans, setting the Hearnes Center dual attendance record.

Over his twenty-six-season tenure at Missouri, Smith has achieved a 336-120-4 record, becoming the first coach in program history to reach 300 wins, a milestone he surpassed on January 8, 2021, with a 30-6 victory over number twenty-one Central Michigan. With a .724 career winning percentage, Smith holds the highest winning percentage in Mizzou wrestling history. Upon Missouri's return to the Big 12 in 2022, Smith earned his second and third Big 12 Coach of the Year honors, in 2022 and 2023, having first received the award in 2012. During Missouri's time in the Mid-American Conference (MAC), Smith won five consecutive MAC Coach of the Year honors, from 2013 to 2017.

Smith has been named the top wrestling coach in the NCAA twice in his career, first as the Dan Gable Coach of the Year by *WIN Magazine* in 2007 and later as the NWCA Coach of the Year in 2017. As one of the longest-tenured college wrestling coaches in the country, Smith has earned the respect of his peers nationwide, has served on the NCAA wrestling championship committee, has been a mentor for young college coaches since 2009 through the NWCA Leadership Academy, and was the NWCA president during his time at Missouri.

To contact Brian Smith's team about speaking at your next event, email *BSTigerStyle@gmail.com*.